I0617492

"Dearest Teens,
Thank you for your hard work - expressing your emotions and sharing them, especially in this difficult time during the pandemic of Covid 19. You have done amazing things for your peers and for yourself. Sharing is caring!

Dear Adults,
Love is not enough.
Please, listen and learn from children and teens. This is the best way to help them and all of us during these most difficult times. I cordially recommend the book 6 Feet Apart and the path the teens took by sharing their stories. It can become a crucial way of preventing mental health concerns. Expressing our emotions in our own way is therapeutic and sharing them is a gift to all of us!"

Associate Professor Dr. Mira Polazarevska
Child and Adolescent Psychiatrist
International Balkan University
Republic of North Macedonia

"In the past year, the corporate world has experienced heightened emotional upheavals from the COVID-19 pandemic. One would think leaders and adults around the world would have developed a coping mechanism. This book, written by teenagers, captures five core emotions—anxiety, fear, anger, sadness, and happiness. Noah and his colleagues demonstrate an awareness of their feelings and their ability to communicate and manage them in times of distress. This team of teenagers have produced a book that appeals to all demographics, provoking thoughts on how people worldwide can deal with emotions. Indeed, it is a platform for all of us, especially young people, to learn, connect, and address our emotional experiences even beyond the pandemic, including emotions from wars, famine, abuse, etc."

Jean Claude Abeck
President, Africa Center for Strategic Progress

"This amazing book is such a necessary resource for children, teachers and parents at a very sensitive time when COVID spins everyone's emotions beyond control. Reading what children have gone through and how they have dealt with the 6 feet heartache and pain at so many levels in a world that no longer makes sense should make us all more aware, sensitive, enriched and encouraged. I have been blessed to know Susan Shapiro for 2 decades and her presence has touched my life in so many beautiful ways. Her constant and passionate commitment to help others is at work in 6 feet and she gave confidence to the authors to document their emotions and help others in these historic times. Connecting her with Florentin has been a great joy for me and seeing an American-Romanian team doing such valuable and practical work for all us feels my heart."

Nadia Crisan
Executive Director
The Liechtenstein Institute on Self-Determination
School of Public and International Affairs
Princeton University

"The approach taken by the 6 Feet Apart team is distinctively personalized and authentic. Reading this as a teen, I was amazed at the relatability of this book. The perspectives of other kids my age provided me with relief and learning opportunities, unlike so many other books with the same intent. If there is anything that can aid in the struggles endured by teens throughout the pandemic, its other like-minded teenagers sharing and connecting through art, experience, and vulnerability."

Ari Levin, Age 17
Chevy Chase, Maryland

"6 Feet Apart is a fantastic book for teenagers all over the world. I am from South Africa and I know that teenagers there, like all throughout the world are suffering from the trauma of Covid. I highly recommend this book!"

Lauren Prince
South Africa

"6 Ft. Apart is both inspiring and instructional. These youth have given us a beautiful work that is born of isolation and rises above it. But they have given us so much more. They have firmly established the power of connection and the ability of youth to self -organize in response to the challenges they face. They have shown us what it means to have an authentic relationship with adult allies and have succeeded in leaving all who met them a little more positive about our future."

Joanne Cashman. Ed. D.
Education Consultant and former Director of the IDEA Partnership at The National Association of State Directors of Special Education (NASDSE)

"I am so impressed with the Six Feet Apart team who contributed to his book! Eight youth that did not know each other came together to talk about their experience during the pandemic. They wrote a brilliant book about emotions that will inspire other youth and adults across the globe."

Mariola Rosser, Ed.D.
George Washington University

"Thank you to my Nana. Without my Nana's help I couldn't have done this book. She is also an author herself, so she has taught me so much through the process of writing 6 Feet Apart I'm very grateful for that. My Nana would help out when there was a lack of motivation, and she always would demonstrate kindness, no matter the situation or a tough time it would not change who the kind, loving, caring person she is. My Nana was not only a role model when writing this book but a role model in my life."

Noah Shapiro

"Ever since my first contact with the 6 Feet Apart team I was mesmerized by each member. They were so different for each other and yet they managed to get together as a team and work towards building this project. It was truly inspirational to see how some teenagers who've never met each other, gathered their strengths and formed a place where everybody could express their emotions through art, whether that was writing, drawing or music.

Our weekly meetings lead to building up a non-judgemental platform, where we were able to relate to one another. Nevertheless, we were able to explore how we are the same and how we differ, from a cultural point of view. Thus bringing our creativity to another level. I am really thankful to have met such open minded and empathic people.

For me personally, the experience of writing these paragraphs was therapeutic and it felt like a great introspection period of time. Reading and catching up with my colleagues really strengthened our bond. Knowing how they perceive certain emotions, finding out about their experiences and acknowledging similarities really managed to get the team together."

Ștefania Butucaru
Student at Transylvania College
Public Relations Director, ThinkUp Academy

"In a post-pandemic world, 6 Feet Apart is an important resource for youth to understand and navigate emotional intelligence. Hearing from other young people about mental health can be transformative in encouraging positive behaviors, especially in using mindfulness to help deal with the anxieties of the modern world."

Shruthi Kumar
Student at Harvard College
Founder of GoYogi, a non-profit organization dedicated to increasing access to proactive and preventative mindfulness-based mental health resources.

"As a student who has experienced the isolation and hardships of school during a pandemic I can say that 6 Feet Apart is an important and valuable resource for students to use to manage stress and learn emotional intelligence. Resources like this that encourage mindfulness are extremely important right now because they can help students by learning to face and deal with the anxieties of the world!"

Bethy Belai
Student at Johns Hopkins university

"I have a particular interest in culture and connecting people internationally, and it has been my pleasure to witness all of the hard work that this team has put into developing their resources on emotions to connect students around the globe. Books such 6 Feet Apart are so pivotal for students especially at this time because it promotes emotional intelligence and healthy coping mechanisms. Additionally, it conveys these messages in a real, relatable fashion do students around the world can know that they are not alone."

Kayli Fromm
Student at North Carolina State university

"Covid 19 appeared in the beginning of 2020 and changed the whole world.

It pushed us to alter our lives and as nobody was prepared, it brought a lot of sorrow, feelings of loneliness, fear, anxiety, frustration, panique, depression...

We had to keep our distance from each other even though our planet was so much interconnected. Humankind had a common enemy. As the movement outside was restricted in many countries, adults had to work from home or lose their job. So many problems...

And what about the children?

They "just" did not have to go to school... the wish of many of them fulfilled.

But was it really like what they wanted and needed?

Maybe this interpretation was valid the first moment, but it did not take a lot of time and kids had to face the same negative feelings as we did. After some time they began to miss their social contact. They began to miss their previous life and their emotional health began to suffer.

How many knew how to express their feelings? How many of them understood their emotions?

We now know many children are anxious, many have PTSD. Were we aware of their emotional health before COVID? How much...

COVID actually gave us the possibility to take their feelings seriously.

Let us use it now.

6 Feet Apart is very valuable. It is not written just by adults, experts. It is written by Noah and his friends under the sensitive leadership of his Nana. What a great opportunity!

We do not know what the future brings, but our one expert who explores the brain, František Koukolík, says: Man is a ball of emotion, which sometimes decides intellectually.

Let this great book help our kids (not only) in emotional development (but in understanding, expressing and working with their feelings).

This book is an opportunity for positive change."

Vera Janikova
Former special pedagogue, Health Education Director and Trainer offering health programs and workshops to thousands of teachers across the Czech Republic, Health Education Specialist

Ivan Janik, Psychologue
Former Principal of Special School for Children with handicaps, Teacher Trainer of Health Education offering workshops to thousands of teachers, Novy Jicin, Czech Republic

6 FEET APART

The Curve of Five Emotions

by

Noah Shapiro

6 FEET APART TEAM
NOAH, EDIE, CASSANDRA, SAMANTHA,
ASIA RAE, JULIA, AMANI, ELIF

Coaches
SUSAN SHAPIRO, DR. SALLY BAAS,
SIMONA BACIU

Copyright © 2023 Tapestry Intergenerational Education Foundation (TIEF)
All rights reserved.
No part of this book may be reproduced without written permission from
Tapestry Intergenerational Education Foundation.

ISBN: 979-8-9860574-1-5

Contents

Welcome to Our World

You Have Just Entered
The World Of Positive Change...

6 Feet Apart is written by Noah Shapiro, age 14, with collaboration from seven of us who are all teenagers. Noah began writing it with his grandmother in early March, 2020 as the coronavirus entered his town of Lexington, Massachusetts. He noticed that he couldn't provide all that he thought was important. He said to his Nana, "The book needs other kids' perspectives, not just mine". They asked teenagers to add their voice through art, music, poetry, sports, photography and layout design. They found us through family, friends and professional contacts. Noah's first question was, "What would you want to contribute?" We all answered with almost the same message. "We want to help other teenagers understand how this pandemic has affected them and we want to express ourselves through our own creativity."

Along with Noah, we dedicated our time to do just that. We created artwork, designed the layout, included photography, composed music especially depicting our moods during COVID, and wrote poems. Our team consists of Noah, Cassandra, Edie, Samantha, Asia Rae, Julia, Amani and Elif. We also want to thank Nathan Schwartz who gave us his brilliant art to include in the book.

We want to help you understand the pandemic - but in our case, through the eyes of all of us as teenagers. Our work is based on five emotions we have felt during COVID: fear, anxiety, anger, sadness and happiness. Noah created a Five Emotions Survey based on these emotions so we have data from others across the globe showing how others felt.

Through our experience we have learned what it means to be productive and a contributing asset to a project bigger than any one of us, forming an effective, efficient, and collaborative team. Even though we come from diverse backgrounds and haven't met in person we have helped each other and we formed relationships that continue today. We have created a sense of belonging and that has helped us feel connected during COVID.

As you read 6 Feet Apart, think about the changes you have had to make: you have to stand six feet apart: you are supposed to isolate yourself from your friends; you have to wear a mask and if you are like us, you have to spend far more time at home than you had ever imagined.

We all have had to adjust to changes that we never could have ever imagined, experiencing a challenge no one has faced in our lifetime. Our parents haven't gone through this and our teachers haven't either. No one alive has.

We will continue to face more challenges. Our schools aren't the same, learning isn't the same. We don't know what to expect from one day to the next. But when we understand our feelings, we can break the cycle of fear, anxiety, anger and sadness. We hope this book gives you such an opportunity.

The book focuses on our emotions during the pandemic. As you read about our experience, you are given the opportunity to create your own story, an important step towards understanding your circumstances. Within our stories we shared our emotions which were often hard to disclose, especially to you, as readers, whom we have never met. But we found that when we express ourselves, we let go of some of the negative emotions and embrace more happiness. We hope this happens to you as well, as you delve into our experiences and yours

We have created Virtual Museum of Arts and Science to explore the analytical and emotional perspectives. It is a presentation of the COVID period that includes the results from the Five Emotions Survey; information about the historical context of the pandemic; our bios; a music and art guide to help you understand our own works; a guide for teachers and parents, and various other things that we hope contribute to the history of this pandemic. Welcome to our world!

The 6 Feet Apart Team
Noah, Edie, Cassandra, Samantha,
Asia Rae, Amani, Julia, Elif

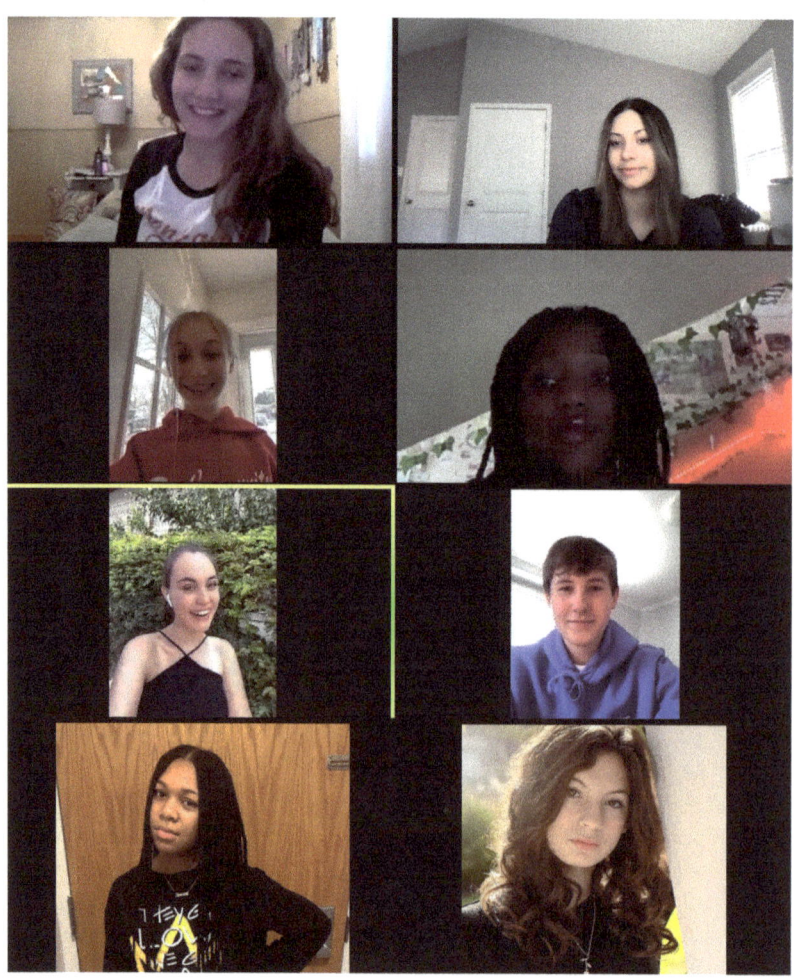

Team Bios

Noah Shapiro
Author

My name is Noah Shapiro and I am the author of this book. You'll hear more about me throughout this book but here's my short introduction. My birthday is August 27, 2005, and I am 14 years old. I was born right during the Katrina Hurricane. I've lived in Massachusetts my whole life. Before the coronavirus I would go into downtown Lexington with my friends. I am standing in the town in my picture. I am the oldest child in my family and my brothers are Zach and Liam.

I love sports. It is my passion. I play on different soccer teams. My position on the field is left back. I have learned so much from playing on soccer teams and have grown as a person through soccer.

Through the social aspect and playing competitive soccer, I have created a life that was great for me. Even this book began when I was in the car with my Dad driving back from a soccer practice, 10 PM one night, and I had this idea to write a book about five emotions, and how to understand them so you can use them and be the best you can be. I told my Dad about my idea and he liked it. He's an author, so he knew what it was like to write a book. Time went by and soccer and school took over.

But it was about a month later, the coronavirus struck and that's when I had to change my lifestyle because we were quarantined. I got the urge to write this book even more, the emotions I had thought about, and that were now part of most people's lives and affecting all of us. So I started writing it and I would call my Nana and we brainstormed the ideas.

The ideas grew as the coronavirus grew. I decided that pictures would make the book so much more hooking so we found two students from Pennsylvania, Edie and Cassandra, who loved to draw through Nana's best friend, Joan who lives in Harrisburg, PA. Edie is her granddaughter and Cassandra lives across the street from Joan. Then other artists - all teenagers - appeared. Again through Nana's friends and colleagues. Samantha, a student in the Washington DC area whose mother is Nana's colleague, and two students from New Jersey, Julia and Amani. Julia's mom, Randi, is friends with my Aunt Maddie. Then we thought that we would like to include music. And we connected through my Aunt Margaret with a student, Asia Rae from Pittsburgh, PA. I read her bio and she's amazing. Elif appeared later and she has added another dimension to our book since she is a student at American University and not able to even be on campus because of COVID. We are a team and we have bonded. A few of us have met in person, but most haven't. But we will. We are all connected to this book. Let me introduce you now to the leader of our team, Edie. Without her leadership, this book would not be what it has become. Edie is organized and when she says she will do something, it gets done. Here's Edie.

Edie Myhre
Artist, Editor, Research Consultant
and Photographer

Hello ! My name is Edie Myhre and I am a junior at Red Land high school outside of Harrisburg, PA. In school, I am a member of the Golf team, I am a junior class officer, part of the Mini Thon committee, and serve on the executive board of Key Club, which is a student-led volunteer organization. Outside of school I have earned my black belt in martial arts, and love to spend time taking classes and teaching at my studios. In my free time, I love to run, play piano, and spend time with family and friends. I am very grateful for the opportunity to be a part of creating this book, because it has allowed me to make lots of wonderful connections, and allowed me to express myself creatively during quarantine. It was such a unique and fun experience, to take someone else's story, and animate it and bring it to life as best I could, and find fun and creative ways to represent and articulate the messages throughout the story with pictures and design. Through this book, I also had the opportunity to research adverse childhood experiences, positive childhood experience, resilience, risk and protective factors, and the benefits of education on "trauma informed schools and communities" under Doctor Joanne Cashman. My research dives into the negative mental, emotional and physical tolls trauma and unhealthy adversity has on children; which is why I am passionate about using resources such as this book to help schools and communities better understand, connect, and engage their youth. Additionally, by providing youth with information on how to positively and productively deal with trauma and emotions I can do my small part in helping to break the trauma to trauma cycle in homes, schools, and communities. This process of illustrating the book has positively impacted me, because it was extremely eye opening when I looked at the results of the survey, and realized everybody, no matter who they are, or where they are from, is going through the same thing and feeling common emotions. I believe that the book will create a sense of much needed unity to everyone whom the book reaches. Let me introduce you to Cassandra, my dear friend. I know her on and off Zoom!!! Cassandra loves to be social. She spent time doing the artwork, and added so much positive energy to our team. She is the only person who I actually have seen in real life!! All the others, I can't wait to meet in person.

Cassandra Zart
Artist, Designer and Editor

Hello happy readers! I am Cassandra Zart and I am 15 years old! I am currently a 9th grader at Susquehanna Township High School in Harrisburg, Pennsylvania. I am one of the illustrators for this amazing book. I got involved with this project as my Best Friend Edie (Co-illustrator) asked if I would like to be a part of it, since she knows I like to draw. I like to play field hockey, work-out/go running, watch Penn State football, go swimming, hang out with family and friends, sing and dance. I also like to go to church and church events and participate in school activities such as the Key club and student government. This project impacted me in a positive way. I was able to turn what people are feeling/doing during this COVID 19 pandemic into artwork. It was a way I could visualize what is happening in the world around me. Apart from the pandemic, I was able to make and gain new remarkable friends. This project allowed me to relax and be creative. Especially during a crazy and scary time, drawing was a great escape. My big inspiration for this book is that this will be my first ever book that I was a part of that got published! Furthermore, it is exciting that it was a team effort by studious, talented, and creative teenagers (with help from Susan). A little description of my artwork...I like to draw cartoons. I like making my artwork fun! Art is not my first career path, but I love doodling! The path that I'm thinking of taking is Communication and Journalism so being a part of a project for a published book is great to have under my belt! I am beyond thankful for Susan, Noah, Asia Rae, and Edie for giving me this opportunity! I now introduce you to Samantha, or as we call her, Sam. Sam is amazing and her artwork on the cover really shows the complexity of our emotions during COVID. Sam has worked hard with us to make the artwork flow. She also put a lot of energy into each piece of work here. The details of her art are amazing. And Sam really speaks her truth. I want to add one short comment. All of our team members have been kind to one another. We listened, and respected each other and that made us feel good. Now, meet Sam!

Samantha Rosser
Artist, Writer

Hi! My name is Samantha Rosser and I am 16 years old, and currently a sophomore at Maret School in Washington DC. I live with my parents and two dogs. I play volleyball and softball and plan to play volleyball in college. I earned a black belt in karate after doing it for 10 years, starting at the age of 3. I play golf with my dad, go on long nature walks with my mom, and I love coffee!! I have a lot of special talents but my most notable one is my art. I love art. I used to draw all the time when I was younger and evolved to make my art about the world and my experiences. I express myself through art when I can't convey my feelings simply through talking. I am pretty introverted and like to be by myself most of the time, but I am also very social. I do my best artwork when sitting alone in my room, with fresh light peering in from the windows. My favorite is abstract art using paints but I also love drawing and sketching. Art has influenced me during COVID-19. It really is therapeutic to release my anxiety and other feelings. I can spend hours and hours working on painting and feel so much better afterwards. In fact, I did one just last night for my English class, representing American Society. My biggest painting is the one you see on the cover of this book. I am so grateful to Susan for convincing me to be involved with something that will impact so many people, and to my mom for bringing this project to my attention. I'm excited for the opportunity to share my artwork along with many other talented kids! I would now like to introduce you to someone in our group who really is special. Her name is Asia Rae and she is an amazing musician. I remember when I first heard her song that she wrote for this book. You must listen to it. It is exceptional. She plays so many instruments and still has time for homework and for our team. Welcome her!!! She is the girl without the mask in the picture. She has the best smile ever!

Asia Rae Smith
Musician, Creator of 6 Feet Apart Song
and Graphic Designer

Hello to everyone reading this! I'm Asia-Rae and I am 13 years old in 8th grade. I attend CAPA performing arts school in Pittsburgh Pennsylvania. I wrote the song for the book "6 Feet Apart". I used my keyboard to write and play the piece and it really shows my overall emotions and feelings during this global pandemic. I have been musically inclined since I was 4 years old. As of now I play ten instruments. Those instruments being the violin, viola, harp, piano, ukulele, bass, guitar, vibraphone, cello, and flute. Music is something that created the person I am today. Besides music I enjoy science, specifically earth and space sciences. Before the pandemic I was getting ready for orchestral performances and looking forward to a trip to New York. Although this has taken a lot from me it has also brought attention to many things I haven't thought of before. It has also created many complications with people around me. Doing things has become a lot harder. And my motivation to continue doing things has left me distraught. Being involved with this book has brought new people and friends into my life. Even though we are from all walks of life, we have come together to create something brilliant. And now it is my turn to introduce Julia to you. Her artwork you will see for yourself is truly unique. She can express her emotions so clearly through art. Julia spends time listening to music, but when she paints or draws, you can see the emotions she is feeling in her artwork. I am so glad she is part of The 6 Feet Apart Team. Hi to Julia!

Julia Goldstein
Artist

Hello. My name is Julia Goldstein and I am 12 years old and a 6th grade student living in Livingston, NJ. Prior to COVID-19, I enjoyed playing soccer and basketball for my town and school. I enjoyed spending my weekends hanging out with my friends and family. I also like to sing, draw and listen to music.

When the pandemic started, I didn't think it would affect the world as deeply as it has but it did. My life has changed drastically and was flipped upside down. The drawings that I created are based on my thoughts and experiences while being quarantined. I had to find a new normal through virtual learning and hang outs and a different way to express myself artistically. I hope you enjoy the book and find comfort in knowing that through these hard times, you're not alone. I would like to introduce you to Amani. She is both an artist and a poet and I think you will see her exceptional talent in both. Amani is not afraid to express how she truly feels. You will recognize her ability in the poem she wrote: I Can't Breathe! Welcome Amani!

Amani Simon
Artist and Poet

Hi, my name is Amani Simon. I am a 14- year- old 9th grader at West Orange High School. Prior to Covid-19 I played for my school's volleyball team, and was hoping to start lacrosse this spring. I was also looking forward to a trip to Lincoln Center with my Honors History and English classes. Life was great! I enjoyed shopping, movies and football games with my friends, and trips to my favorite ice cream shop with my mom and brother.

Covid-19 has somehow taken that all away. I created my drawing to express my deepest thoughts during this pandemic. It is my hope that I will encourage others to express their fears and not suppress them. I believe that self expression is healthy and necessary during these scary times. I hope my drawing encourages other kids my age to do the same. Never be afraid to be vulnerable, never be afraid to show the world the real you! I welcome Elif, our newest member of the team. Her writing is deep and reflective. I haven't had much time to get to know Elif, but her writing and artwork tell me much about her. Hi Elif and welcome!

Elif Ak
Writer, Leader and Team Mentor

Hello everyone!

My name is Elif Ak and I am the author of the story "The Spectrum of Life" in the book 6 Feet Apart! I am an undergraduate student at American University studying Data Sciences in Justice Law and Criminology but I am interested in adding International Relations as a double major. I am nineteen years old and I'm completing my first year of college, remotely, in the city I currently reside in, Sarasota, Florida. I was born and raised in Istanbul, Turkey and I moved to the United States when I was twelve years old. I was challenged to learn the English language as a beginner and I am proud of the progress I've made throughout the years. I am so happy to share my story on emotions "Happiness and Hope". My story highlights all five emotions that many of my peers have faced during the pandemic but it has a happy ending that reflects the importance of hope and choosing to be happy every single day. It was a very sincere story on how I felt and the challenges I've faced during the past year. It is an honor to be able to tell my story and reflect back on my growth during the COVID-19 pandemic.

I am the last member of this team. We are about to begin our story of **COVID** and we want you to know it is hard to write our emotions. You may feel the same way. One of us, and this person is anonymous, but a member of the 6 Feet Apart Team, decided to write a piece you are about to read, without a name on it. They were more comfortable writing this way. You too may feel that you don't want your name on your writing - or on your artwork. That's okay. We want you to express yourself in the way that fits you the best. So read Endless Cycles by Anonymous...

Endless Cycles By Anonymous 1/10/21

Endless Cycles. It's the same thing over and over again. You'd think that it'll be easy, but it's draining. I'm so lost in motivation. Stuck in my head as much as I'm stuck in my house. Seeing the same faces every day, confined to 2D screens of faces, lacking physical touch, craving to be freed from this prison. Everyone clings to the hope of things being normal. But can't get out of romanticized moment to see how broken they are. Sipping down that sugar coated version of how to cope. And at the same time, reality slips away. But it's close enough for you to secure your grip and come to terms with what's really going on. Being brave enough to share how you really feel, is the first step to our fantasy of a "normal ". And yes, it's easier said than done. It's easier to lie and say everything is ok. Or to tell people what you want them to know. Yes, there are some things that aren't meant to be said out loud to just anyone. In this situation, no one is alone. Physically we are isolated. But mentally and emotionally we are standing together. Being vulnerable isn't weakness, in most cases it's strength. Being hard on yourself gets to a point where you degrade your self worth. Not only should we be kind to others, but to ourselves as well. Suppressing feelings and pent up issues doesn't benefit anyone. The mentality that not telling someone something means that they are better off is so wrong. Bettering yourself by speaking your truth, is the first step to healing.

"THE ENTIRE WORLD IS CONNECTED THROUGH THIS VIRUS. NO MATTER WHO YOU TALK TO ACROSS THE GLOBE, WE ARE ALL EXPERIENCING THE SAME THING. YET, I HAVE NEVER FELT SO ISOLATED!"

ASIA RAE SMITH
talking to The Team on Zoom,
April, 2020

An Idea That Turned Into Something So Big!
By Noah

It's important for me to share how this project developed. As I already told you, this is the first book I have ever written, and it raised many different emotions. Without my Nana's help, there would be no way I could have written it. Our process went something like this: every afternoon at around 1 pm I would call my Nana or she'd call me. We'd catch up on each other's lives, then work on the book. I didn't always want to work on it. I sometimes wanted to play soccer or talk on my phone. But I did it anyway (most of the time).

In the early stages of writing, I had some basic ideas and would sit in my room on my Chrome computer and write out everything that came to mind. Nana and I would talk through the ideas and brainstorm what each chapter would be about. Word by word, page by page, chapter by chapter, the book evolved. And it got better. I started to understand more about how to write, and I started to learn more about fear, anxiety, anger, sadness and happiness.

Once everything started to come together, we would add as much detail as we could. I would write at least one page every day, with as much detail as I could. Nana would look it over and we would edit it on the phone the next day. Sometimes she would help me expand on an idea and write that text with me. We would create the meditations, question sheets and calming exercises together, but it was Nana who took the lead there because that's what she teaches.

Most of the time what she and I did varied: helping me to write, getting me to expand on an idea, or motivating the team to make this book so much better. When working on this book I could see my writing skills improve and I could understand how to make a book more appealing to the readers by hooking them in and giving a lot of detail when expanding something. Writing a book is a lot harder than I thought and it is crazy to think that this one idea turned into something so big.

Chapter One - **Anxiety**

Artwork of the Emotions Wheel by Cassandra

Anxiety Is a Chatterbox!
It Doesn't Stop Talking...

I was a normal kid with a normal life. Sometimes I was angry. Sometimes I was sad. Sometimes I was afraid too. Until the coronavirus appeared in my life, I didn't think so much about my emotions.

I would experience them and I am interested in emotions, but I didn't dwell on one emotion over another. But then COVID appeared and everyone started saying they were anxious. That's the first emotion most people said and it puzzled me.

Artwork by Samantha

Anxiety was not an emotion I felt. It happened to others. I didn't think of myself as anxious. Math tests, soccer games and just other everyday stuff can make me uncomfortable. But I didn't associate it with anxiety. That is until I started writing this book and so many people said they were anxious.

I examined the word anxiety and realized that we all have it at some point in our lives. It sure is happening now during this pandemic. Many people are anxious. Let me share what I have discovered.

Artwork by Edie

I heard the word anxiety about the coronavirus used on the news, by my teachers, with my parents, and it seemed to be mentioned everywhere. Yet I didn't think I was anxious because of this virus. Some people said they felt fear, but why is everyone saying they are anxious? Those were the words I heard most often when the virus first appeared in my life.

My Nana who is helping me write this book said she was anxious. "I don't know what is going to happen with this virus," she told me. Then she asked me, "Noah, are you anxious about the virus?" I replied, "NO!" It was a loud no. I didn't feel it.

"When have you felt anxious?"

"Never," I answered.

She said, "We all get anxious. Think about it. Do you know what anxiety means?" I looked it up in the dictionary and it said that *anxiety is your body's natural response to stress. It's a feeling of fear or apprehension about what's to come.* That definition wasn't much help, so I asked Nana for some examples. She said, "Think about how you felt on the first day of school. Or when you take an important test, or give a speech to your class, or play for the soccer championship."

Sure, I thought, I get sort of nervous, like am I going to do okay? With that definition I guess I have had anxiety. I went back in time to a situation where I definitely felt anxious.

"Nana, I remember an incident where I was definitely anxious, and you were a part of it." Here's what happened to me and my family. I hope this story gets you thinking about when you get anxious.

I was almost nine years old and, along with my father and brother Zach, we went to my grandparents' house in Washington DC. It was summer, 2014. My Mom couldn't go on this trip with us so it was just us boys. My youngest brother Liam wasn't born yet. We loved going hiking in Rock Creek Park right behind their house. It's a huge park that goes through Maryland and D.C.

We flew on JetBlue and got to their house about four hours after we left our own home. We were excited to be with Nana and Papa because they always had fun things for us to do. Nana packed a bag of "goodies" for us wherever we went. Ten minutes after we walked into their house, my Papa said, "Let's go for a walk in the woods. We can eat a quick lunch and then go exploring." He meant Rock Creek Park but they call it "the woods". It is huge, with creeks and thousands of trees and paths that go on for miles. Hundreds of rocks, all kinds. There are cement paths and dirt paths, and bridges that take you further into the woods. We love going there. We have the Minuteman Trail down the street from our house, but it's different from their woods. Rock Creek is more isolated with far more trees.

It was a humid, sunny summer day, and in Washington the summers are *really* humid. Mosquitos are out and all kinds of insects swarm the air. Papa and my Dad weren't quite ready to go because they were still eating lunch, but I, my Nana and my brother Zach didn't want to wait. Zach and I had been sitting too long and now wanted to run through the woods. So Nana said, "I'll take the boys and we'll meet you on the trail." We walked out their back door and toward the woods, holding our "goodie bags" filled with lollipops, Cheez-its and animal crackers. Their neighbor, Kent, was outside his house and after meeting us, decided to come along.

We headed into the woods and my Nana said, "Last week when Jake (my cousin) was here, he took a quarter and hid it in a fallen tree. The tree is off the path and deep in the woods, but I bet we can find it." Zach and I liked the idea. It was a real challenge to find Jake's quarter and then Nana said we could add ours. She handed each of us a quarter.

"Can you find the same tree?" I asked Nana.

"Yes," she said. "I sort of know where it is. I remember I had to stumble over branches and hoped I wouldn't see a snake! The tree is huge and lying on its side. Jake chose it because it was the biggest tree he could find with thick roots. He wanted to walk across the top of it, but we didn't have time."

Nana, Zach, Kent and I searched for about five minutes and then we found the tree and walked toward it.

"I can't find Jake's quarter," I said. Zach wasn't as interested at this point and said he would wait at the path for us.

"Keep looking," Nana said, "it's somewhere near the edge there."

"Oh, there it is! Jake's quarter," I said, so excited to find where Jake put it. I placed my quarter right next to his.

Artwork by Cassandra

All of a sudden Kent spotted moss on the tree and lifted it up. At that second, hundreds of hornets flew out toward us.

Kent screamed, "They're hornets! Everybody run!!!"

Zach was already running down the hill and away from us. Nana was running toward me. I ran as fast as I could, the hornets chasing after us as I looked back and saw Kent and my Nana running at full speed, hornets attacking and stinging them. We were screaming on the top of our lungs. Nana told me later she was scared to death that I was allergic to hornets. But I was okay.

My Dad and Papa were walking into the woods and heard us yelling. They thought we were laughing. My Dad screamed, "Where are you guys?" But we were still running for our lives. Then they spotted us and saw we weren't laughing. They were shocked. We were so scared, Nana hurting, Kent covered with hornets. I learned afterward that hornets can sting you over and over again. They kept doing that to Nana.

We all survived, but not without anxiety that this could happen again in the future. Nana had almost 30 hornet stings which made her feel anxious for years. She wouldn't go off the trail near fallen trees. She is still afraid of hornets. Kent had over 50 bites with hornets stuck in his hair. I got eight sting bites. They all went in my hair. We went back to their house and Kent, having knowledge of natural remedies, helped us treat the stings.

Again, the actual hornet swarming and stinging produced fear in us. We ran as fast as we could to protect ourselves. Then anxiety appeared. Nana said, "Now, I feel anxious every time we hike past the tree where the hornets are nesting. I will never get close to that tree again!!! I will never forget the feeling of running through the woods escaping the hornets."

It's almost seven years later and I still remember it. It was a scary experience for all of us. The fear has not lasted , but the anxiety has.

Let me tell you what I think about anxiety in regard to this virus. At first, we did not understand what this coronavirus, Covid-19, was all about and most people did not seem to believe it could ever affect us here in the U.S. This caused people to be anxious. *They had a feeling of apprehension of what's to come,* as it said in the dictionary. There was uncertainty.

I don't think I had much anxiety at first until the threat of this virus hurting me or my family became more real. My Nana's friend, Joan, described the difference between fear and anxiety to me. "Remember when you were walking in the woods and the hornets jumped out and stung you. It was an observable, clear and present danger. That's fear," Joan said. "But anxiety is when your Papa asks you to walk in the woods the next day and you are not only afraid that you might see another hornet's nest, but you are now worried about how awful the situation was for you. You are feeling anxious and so you don't even want to go walk in the woods with your grandfather."

Same as the virus. When people heard about the virus, some got anxious. They got anxious worrying about the future in general. What is going to happen to me? How would I deal with something like this? How am I going to deal with future uncertainty?

When I think of anxiety during COVID, I think of my school work a little, but in a way, my unconscious self gets anxious when I think of soccer. Soccer is most important to me. It wasn't like I thought that I would not play as well, or I would become rusty. It wasn't a conscious thought over and over again in my head. It was a part of me that I wanted to succeed in soccer and when I am not playing for a great amount of time, I felt it might worsen me as a player and that's what I didn't want. It wasn't fear. I think it was anxiety. Maybe I didn't know what anxiety felt like before Nana and I discussed it, or before COVID. I never had that feeling happen before. I wonder if other teenagers felt something new with this feeling of anxiety.

I didn't know if any of you felt this way too. Were you afraid? Anxious? What was going on inside of you? I suggested to Nana that we create a Survey that asks others how they felt. I thought about the emotions that are most important to me and I named them: Anxiety, fear, anger, sadness and happiness too. I wrote up a Survey and we put it online. It was really fun looking at how other people felt. We kept getting results. I made it and sent it to people of all ages.

If you want to, look in the back pages of this book and you will see the entire Survey and the results. I asked people five questions - one about each emotion. I had never done anything like this before, but I knew what I wanted to find out. I wanted to know how others were feeling, simple as that. So I created questions asking what I hoped to learn. Nana and I sent it out to everyone we knew. My Dad and Mom sent it to some of their colleagues and then my relatives also helped get it out.

The Survey confirmed to me and to Nana that many teenagers didn't go through this anxiety emotion. Maybe they were like me and didn't know what anxiety felt like. From the Survey we found that more adults felt anxious. Kids, of course, felt something, but they didn't label it anxiety. Nana and I talked about it often. She would ask me over and over again, "Aren't you feeling anxious?" I kept saying no. I really wasn't. Maybe this virus is now making us anxious.

I was amazed when I started to get results back. The answers confirmed my thinking - there was so much similarity in all of us, no matter our age or our gender. I started comparing the data. People worldwide, no matter their occupation, age, gender, language, or country were experiencing these same feelings. We received almost 500 responses from people in 18 different countries. The data includes the countries, the range of occupations, the ages, gender, etc. I am fascinated with it and I think most of you will be too.

Here's a map showing the locations of the many participants.

Map drawn by CODEX team.

I found it incredible that no matter whether it was an 11 year old student living in Rwanda or an 86 year old man in the United States or a teacher in Canada, we all felt fear, anger, anxiety, sadness, and happiness! Some were more anxious than afraid. Others were more afraid than anxious. Some were more sad, but everyone was feeling some of these five emotions. But most adults were anxious.

I guess anxiety is something many of us don't agree upon, or don't see in ourselves. Yet others see it in us. I thought my Dad was anxious, but he said he wasn't. It may sound confusing but I wonder if sometimes we express how we feel in different ways. Maybe the word anxiety sounds negative and he doesn't want me to label him. I still wonder if teenagers get it less than adults. I still think so.

Artwork by Cassandra

So the virus spread and became a real physical threat to all of us. We were on a house lockdown. We began to spray down or wash every box delivered to our house and everything that we bought at the store. We didn't go to the store -- we'd get our groceries delivered. This continued for three months after the virus hit.

During this time, I continued to think my Dad was anxious. I asked him and he said, "No. I am trying to protect all of us from the virus to keep us safe." I think he really was anxious. But it's not my right to label him. I guess it is up to each of us to own our emotions. I know when Nana asked me if I was anxious, I said no. She thought I was and I kept saying no I am not. It's important you do not assume you know someone else's feelings. You really don't. You might think you do, but ask, and might find you were wrong.

The Survey was a good indicator of how people labeled themselves. Because anxiety is the most confusing emotion to me, I found it hard to believe it was the number one emotion people felt. And that's why we made it Chapter One. But when we looked closely at the data, we saw that many teenagers had fear and some had anxiety. Adults felt more anxious and showed less fear. It is about being uncertain about what is going to happen. Either way, as the Coronavirus spread anxiety spread. Here are some teenagers' comments. There are more comments in the back of the book about this Survey. You also go to our Virtual Museum online and find out even more about emotions. To view the full version of The Five Emotions Survey, please go to the back of the book (See pages 179-198). See for yourself! People label their emotions differently, but most of us feel them in the same way.

COMMENTS ON ANXIETY

- "Because I have no idea what will happen tomorrow" - 13 years old student

- The uncertainty of the situation because it is unprecedented" - 17 years old student

- "Uncertainty about the future of school and the country" - 18 years old student

- "Having to stay inside in quarantine all the time and worry about adjusting to online school/quarantine life." - 19 years old student

- "We have not lived through something like this before in such a modern world. We have the tools to flatten the curve and take care of people but then others won't listen, which creates issues into stopping the spread." - 19 years old student

- "Government inaction, uncertainty about the future, having family members and loved ones at high risk, and little personal control over the situation." - 21 years old college student

If you feel some anxiety, you aren't alone. Look at this chart from the Five Emotions Survey.

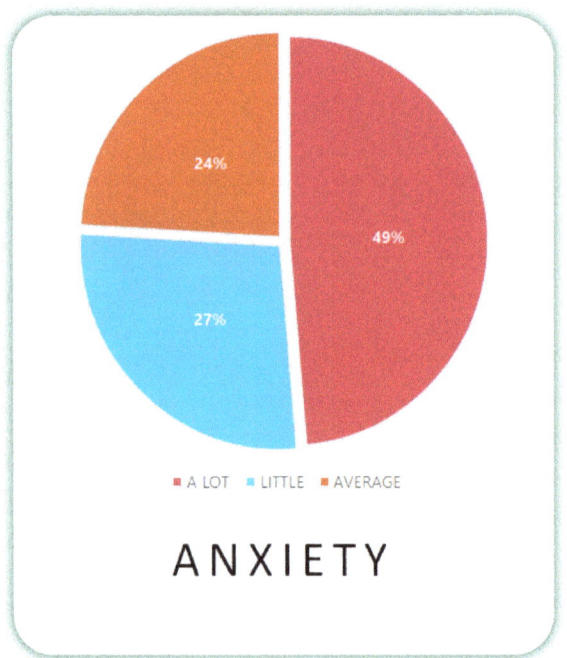

Understanding Why We Get Anxious

These are my conclusions. Anxiety is when you can't get your mind off something and you can't stop thinking about it. There's a feeling of uncertainty. It is connected to fear. My Papa said to me, "You can't separate the two. I feel afraid of the virus and then I get anxious about it. How could it be any different? They are so similar. One leads to the other and then takes over. I am worried about the future - for you guys, my grandchildren. I don't want you to be isolated without your friends." I think he is an expert on anxiety, because he worries a lot. But he worries about all of us.

Artwork by Cassandra

As I examine anxiety, I must admit that I get anxious at times. I just didn't realize it. I remember when I had a math test and I was afraid I would get a bad grade. I had studied and I

knew the material. I had no reason to get anxious because I knew it. But before the math test, doubt occurred and then anxiety set in. I said to myself, "I shouldn't be nervous because I know I know it!!!"

Artwork by Edie

But I started doubting myself, because I wanted to get a good grade. And in this type of situation you get too much inside your head. So to me, anxiety is usually overthinking. My brain becomes overwhelmed with thoughts. If they took an MRI of my brain, it would look like a wild, crazy party.

I now know more about anxiety since I started reading about it and writing this book. Now that I know what anxiety really is, I know my body reacts to it. I can get butterflies in my stomach, or a headache or even nausea. Think about how you feel when you get anxious.

When I took that math test, back when I was in school, I got into the classroom, got the test in front of me and because I knew it, my anxiety went away. But it was because I knew it. I had studied. If I hadn't studied, I wouldn't perform as well, and the anxiety could go up. The more prepared I am, the less anxiety I feel. That's because I have more certainty about what I know.

If you make a mistake or you are uncertain of the future you might get anxious. But anxiety comes in different ways for different people and we all can respond to it in different ways. I think my Dad is anxious when he gets too many emails and when he has too much work and definitely when he is sleep deprived.

When he is really anxious, he spends time with me and my brothers, going outside and shooting baskets, or he goes on his bike alone on the Minuteman Trail. My Papa gets anxious when he watches too much of the news. Especially during COVID 19. He gets annoyed when people don't wear masks or when they get too close to him when he is walking. Maybe as you read this, you will feel that you too get anxiety at times.

We all do. Now I am aware of when it happens to me. I sometimes get anxious when others around me are feeling anxious. If my brother is feeling anxious, I feel his energy. Or if I am watching TV and someone on the news had a family member

Artwork by Cassandra

die and they talk about it and I listen, then I feel anxious. I become aware that I am feeling something. Even if I don't know the person, it can make me anxious. Then the anxiety can spread. It's like the anxiety is blowing in the wind. It has its own energy. Just like the virus!!

"YOUR CHALLENGE"
FROM ANXIETY TO FEELING
SOMEWHAT CALMER

1. Know it's okay to feel anxious.

2. Think about what is causing your anxiety.

3. Know what it is doing to your body. Do you feel it in your gut? Or do you get tired?

4. Think about what could make you feel better.

5. Do some artwork, or listen to music. Write a poem. Do something.

6. Sit down and focus on your breath for about three minutes.

7. Go out and exercise.

8. Eat healthy foods.

9. Count to 10 slowly.

10. Know the anxiety will go away.

Artwork by Edie

46

Understanding Why You Are Anxious...

Think about whether you were anxious during the virus. Just like me, you may not have realized you were feeling anxious. If you aren't anxious, answer the questions so you can understand when and if you get anxious.

I feel anxious when....

_____

_____

_____

_____

_____

_____

My body does the following when I get anxious...

_____

_____

_____

_____

_____

How I deal with my anxiety....

_____

_____

_____

_____

_____

_____

My Nana's Ideas to Calm The "Chatterbox"!

Nana teaches people how to relax and feel less stress and be more in control so they get less anxious. Here she gives suggestions on how we can feel less anxious. How do we calm our "chatterbox?"

Be in The Moment

1. Find a comfortable position. Sit on the floor and cross your legs, straight and tall. Make sure you are comfortable. If you aren't, sit in a chair. You don't want your muscles to get tight. You can move around if you have to, but you want to be comfortable.

2. Sit still and breathe. It's best if you breathe in and your belly expands. That way you get oxygen into your body. It's okay for your mind to wander, just go back to your breath.

3. You are going to think thoughts. It's not possible to not think thoughts! You may be thinking, *Am I doing this right? What should I be doing? I'm not doing this right!* Everyone thinks that.

4. Recognize your thoughts and wait for them to pass. You may realize you aren't as anxious. That's it! Feel a sense of calm, and continue to focus on your breath.

5. Breathe for a few minutes until you feel done, then open your eyes.

Pictures Representing Anxiety

You met our team when you read their bios. They are amazing. They have worked hard analyzing every emotion in this book. They discussed ways to release negative emotions through art, music, poetry and dancing. Samantha Rosser, as you read in her bio, lives in the Washington DC area. Here is her picture that she says represents anxiety. We loved it so much we chose it as the cover of our book. We asked Samantha to break up the picture, like she did below, to make it look like the virus is spreading. Can you find a sense of calmness in her picture or do you see anxiety?

›

Nathan is a teenager who has done wonderful artwork. We asked if he would like to add some pictures into this book and he said he would. Here, Nathan chose a different way to express anxiety. Notice what he wrote in the upper left-hand corner. And look at the way he drew the virus.

YOUR TURN!
DRAW **YOUR** PICTURE OF
ANXIETY OR A PICTURE OF
CALMNESS!

Chapter Two - **Fear**

Artwork by Cassandra

Tackling Fear

Once I analyzed anxiety, which wasn't the emotion I felt the most, but I saw it all around me, then I moved into what was happening to me. Now, during the virus, I realized I had fear!

Artwork by Samantha

I first noticed it when I was sitting in my bedroom, my heart pounding. This was not a fantasy. It was not a dream. It was all about the coronavirus, and it was now taking over my life. It was a cloudy Friday afternoon, the 13th of March, 2020. I left my bedroom and walked into our living room and saw Channel 4 NEWS Boston and they were talking about the coronavirus. *It is now actively infecting people in our area and people are dying*. Those were the words I heard. My Mom was out shopping for food and Coronavirus supplies. She and Dad had to make tough decisions on how we should live in these times. I didn't want to believe what the news was saying, that it could get into our house or that kids in school could get it. Sure, I had fear. But I didn't want to believe it. I had two conflicting sides - one whispering it will never come to Boston. The other saying, it's here and it is the end of the world!

None of the newscasters said the word fear. None of my friends said it, either. But I could feel it. Fear was everywhere.

I kept hearing more and more horrible stories on the news. I was seeing people afraid. I couldn't deny it, so I thought about how fear affects me, my family, and my friends.

Fear is an everyday emotion each one of us uses in our lives. If no one had fear, they would do things that were dangerous. So would I. For example, I might want to ride my bike in the middle of the road, but I don't because I fear getting hit by a car. I thought it was safe to play ice hockey. And for many kids, it is. But I had two concussions. So fear overtook my Mom and Dad, and they stopped me from playing. I had headaches from the concussions, and yes, I even had fear. I was thinking it could happen again and I would not be okay. We all have fear. Even babies. When you scream at them, they cry. That's a sign of fear. Fear is normal because we are human.

My fear really began when I realized how many people were dying and how contagious this virus was. I never knew something like this before. At first I didn't want to talk about it with my friends. When I first heard it was coming into the United States, like in early March, I asked my close friend, Andy, as we stood by our lockers ready to walk into my homeroom, "Do you think that school could get cancelled?" He said probably not. "I doubt it would come to Lexington."

Artwork by Cassandra

I breathed a sigh of relief when he said that. But I also thought, "How does he know?" I was just hopeful.

Then the virus, just like my fear, kept getting closer.

I was in my homeroom about a week after Andy said nothing bad would happen, sitting with my two other friends, Gavin and Feo. Here's how our conversation went:

Feo said, "Yo, the ski trip got cancelled." And I looked up surprised, "Really, that's crazy." He then said, "And I don't even know if we are going to get refunds."

I went to Vince, another friend, and said, "The ski trip got cancelled." He didn't even know why. "Cause of Coronavirus," I said. I knew what it was, but this was the first time it hit me. I went home, told my Mom, and went into my room. The fear kept appearing.

The next few days soccer practice and games got cancelled. I missed soccer a lot. Like it all happened at once. It was still March. I have been playing soccer every day of the week -- 5 pm to 7 pm some days and 7:30 pm to 9:30 pm other days. I didn't understand what was going on with this virus. How could it take my life away from me? Especially soccer! Life kept changing. I had been so busy at school, but now I am sitting in my room day after day.

Artwork by Edie

I have my own room at home and am lucky for that. But then I can't stay in my room all day. I was used to my independence and now my Dad started making schedules. I am 14 years old, and I am used to being with my friends, biking over to their houses. I had my freedom. Now I am stuck in the house, either alone in my room or with the rest of my family. And my parents are trying their best, but they keep telling me what to do.

Probably everyone who is reading this can relate to what I'm saying. We all have had to adjust our lives out of fear of contacting the virus. There is no normal anymore.

I read about fear and realized so many of us were feeling this way - adults, teenagers, and even younger kids were scared. There were many reasons for us to feel this fear. We heard news that was extremely frightening and real to us. Our lives were changing. Our parents' lives were changing too. And who knew who would get this virus and who wouldn't. You could not see it, you could not feel it, and you could not describe it.

I started talking to my grandparents more as the virus hit. And I was writing this book with my Nana so we continued our daily writing. I asked her how she would describe fear during this virus. She said, "Once people started getting the virus, people got scared. I don't know anyone who got it...not yet anyhow, but I hear it on the news and it is scary. I became afraid. Fear and anxiety hit so many of us, some didn't realize their fear. Others said they really were afraid.

"Have you heard about what's going on in New York?"

"I heard something but don't know much," I answered.

"Think about the situation there. It is now frightening people across the US and even across the world. There aren't enough beds in hospitals for the very sick. They don't have enough equipment. So people are not only scared about what they are hearing. They are afraid they too might get the virus. Fear isn't just what we feel; our body responds to it too."

I asked Nana, "How does fear affect our bodies?"

She said, "I didn't realize what was going on inside of me when I got scared hearing about the virus. You probably didn't realize what was happening to you because you are focused on dealing with the situation. But when you have fear, your body actually gets ready to defend itself. The pupils in your eyes get bigger and your hearing can become more acute. You are listening to sounds all around you. The fear is giving you signals to protect yourself. The various nervous systems in your body increase your heart rate, your blood pressure, and even your breathing. You breathe faster. The fear prepares your body to fight or flee. If the virus weren't across the entire world, many of us would have wanted to get out of the situation - to flee. We were on high alert."

"Can other people tell if you are afraid?" I asked. I think I'm pretty good at hiding it.

"If you had looked in the mirror, you may have appeared pale because the blood could be flowing away from your skin. Would others see that you were pale? Probably not."

"How do you stop the fear?" I asked.

"I didn't stay in the fear mode for long. I realized I shouldn't watch too much news. I also thought Papa and I would stay inside and be very careful. So we took some action to protect ourselves and that has reduced my fear. I made sure I had the facts about what was happening. And I walked and walked and walked! I made sure to get my exercise and eat healthy foods. I also practiced breathing techniques."

The one fear that dominated all others was my fear that I wouldn't be able to play soccer. It is so important to me. Soccer drives me to improve as a player. When I improve, I get stronger and faster. I have this routine where I do one small thing every day to get better. So it's part of my life. A big part. And if soccer is taken away from me, which it was, it affects other things in my life. It gives me less of a drive to motivate me throughout my day. It isn't only that I am motivated to play soccer, but that motivation goes for everything else; getting good grades and mostly with school work. If you are into sports, you might get the same way. I know my friends on my soccer team do.

So what action could I take so fear wouldn't keep coming to me? I looked again at the Survey and realized we all were feeling the same thing. Here are some of the comments teenagers wrote about their fear. There's more about the Survey in the back of this book and also in the Virtual Museum.

COMMENTS ON FEAR

- "I feel fear because of my family.. I think I will lose them" - 12 year old student

- "Because I have no idea what will happen tomorrow" - 13 year old student

- "Fear that life won't be the same" - 16 year old student

- "The fact that I can't be sure that the moment I come in contact with the virus I won't have the certainty that I'm not going to make anyone else around me sick." - 15 year old student

- "I am not worried about myself, but I am worried about family and friends who may be more vulnerable as a result of their own health complications or a larger risk of being exposed. I tend to stay calm in situations like this, but I still feel fear for families and individuals all around who are or will be negatively impacted by the pandemic." - 19 year old student

Now, look at the circle and you will see that a lot of people felt fear. 33.3% - that's about one in every three people. If you asked three friends if they were afraid, most likely one would say yes. Now, this isn't totally accurate, but it does show me that many of us felt fear.

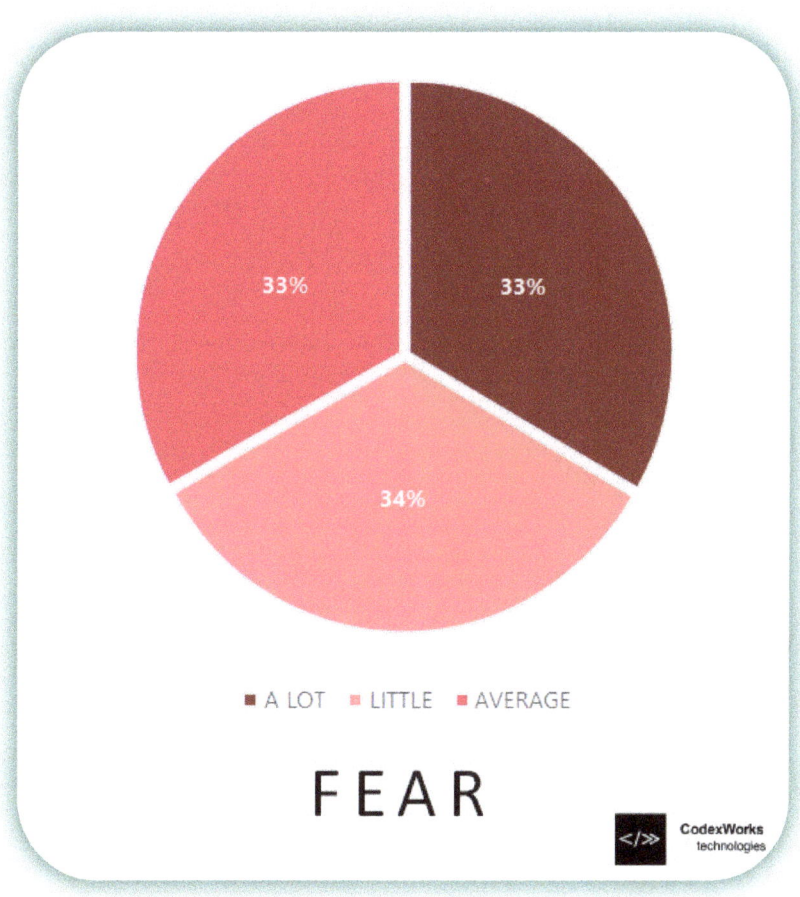

"YOUR CHALLENGE"
FROM FEAR TO A FEELING OF HOPE

I am not the kind of person who likes to have fear or for that matter any negative emotions. My friends would probably say I am happy most of the time. And I was - before COVID. I thought about my challenges and created this list to work on fear, for me or for any of you. Some of the suggestions may not work for you while for others it might help. I would love to hear from you if you have suggestions that could help others. On the next page, you have the opportunity to share your thoughts. It helps to write them down. At least it does for me. I can look them over and when I read my suggestions out loud, I know which ones will work. Here are the ones that I created.

1. Know it's okay to feel fear.
2. Think about what is causing your fear.
3. Know what it is doing to your body. Do you feel it in your gut? Or do you get tired?
4. Think about what could make you feel better.
5. Do some artwork, or listen to music. Write a poem. Do something.
6. Sit down and focus on your breath for about three minutes.
7. Go out and exercise.
8. Think about what makes you hopeful.
9. Do something that makes you feel hopeful.
10. Know the fear will go away

Understanding Why You Are Fearful...

Think about whether you had fear when the virus first hit. Try to figure out why you were afraid. Remember, we all have fear and it's normal.

I first heard about the coronavirus....

_____
_____
_____
_____
_____
_____

The first thing that was taken away from me...

_____
_____
_____
_____
_____
_____

How I deal with fear when I feel it....

_____
_____
_____
_____
_____
_____
_____

My Nana's Ideas To Tackle Fear and Find Hope

My Nana and I talked about fear for many hours. We thought about what was most important to include for you to deal with fear. We finally decided to ask a colleague for helpful information. So Nana had me call an adjunct Professor from University of Virginia, Elyse Conner, who specializes in meditation, mindfulness and techniques that can help teenagers feel better, especially during the pandemic. Elyse helped me understand what was most important when we are dealing with fear. She said, "If you are thinking of fear, are you feeling it in your stomach, heart, or in your back? Where in your body are you noticing a sensation? Then get curious and observe how it feels. Do you feel tightness, tingling, numbness, pins and needles, heaviness, or something else?"

Elyse continued, "Sit with that feeling as long as you can and keep that position and do not get caught up in the reason you feel the fear. And then you will notice that it dissolves. Recognize your fear is going away and don't get caught up in it. Keep still and notice the feelings or sensations in your body."

She also said, "Another way to show your body self-compassion and calm the nervous system is to place *your hand on your heart and allow yourself to feel calm. This calms your peripheral nervous system. Notice how your body responds with the simple gesture and loving tenderness of your hand on your heart. Just sit still, sense your body and breathe. It will help you control your fear.* It can be beneficial to use this technique when you feel uncomfortable. Being non-judgmental is very important. Place your attention on what is happening to you in that moment with intention to gain information about your body, mind, and/or emotions in that moment. Let go of judgment." Elyse gave me the following body scan and I did it several times. It's easy to do when you can't fall asleep at night.

A Body Scan

A body scan can bring your attention to your body and allow you to focus on the fear and know where the fear is. So think about your body and scan it for fear. Start with your feet. Do you feel any fear there? What about your legs? And your stomach? Do you feel fear there? Your arms? Your shoulders? Your hands? What about your face? Your jaw? The back of your head? Where does your fear lie? When you feel fear, sit with it and feel where it is. How does it feel? I repeat the same words again for emphasis on them. Place your hand on your heart and allow yourself to feel calm. If you sit, with your hand on your heart, and breathe, you will feel that you are calm because your peripheral nervous system is calming down. You can sit with the fear too, and put your hand on your heart and breathe. This gives you control of your body. Breathe into the fear. Just sit still and breathe. It will help you control your fear. Sometimes you can't make the fear go away, but when you are aware of it and recognize that fear, it settles you.

Catch A Firefly

Artwork by Cassandra

Nana and I tried to figure out our own method to release fear. Here's what we created together. Fireflies will never be the same to me. Read this simple visualization two times. This will give you the understanding of what we are trying to do. If you could visualize your fear, and then release it, it can help you. But to visualize something like fear at first is hard to do. What does fear look like? So we invented this for you to visualize fear. Nana has used it since we created it and she says it works on her!!

Sit down on the floor or in a chair. Close your eyes and relax. Become still and take three deep breaths. Then think of catching a firefly. You know those fireflies that light up in the summer? Think of one. Imagine that you run to grab it. Visualize that you catch it, place it in your hand and hold onto it. Now pretend that the firefly is afraid and wants you to let it go. You wouldn't want to be this firefly trapped inside someone's palm. So you decide to release it. You set it free. It goes flying away into the night. It is free. It is no longer afraid.

Now think of your fear just like the firefly. You can be free of it too. Think of your fear and then go catch a pretend firefly and hold it in your hand. Continue to hold onto the firefly. You can give it a name if you want. Be clear about your fear. When you are ready, let it go. Then, open your hand, and watch this pretend firefly fly away, carrying your fear with it.

Anytime you have fear, think about this firefly. Breathe and be still. Relax. Catch the firefly, name your fear, feel the firefly in your hand, then when you are ready, let it go. Let your fear fly away. Then you are no longer afraid.

We have given you suggestions on how you can deal with fear. But you may find that you can do something like draw a picture to release your feelings, or go hiking in the woods or play music. There are so many things we can do to release our fear. Our Team did many different things that showed how they dealt with fear. We talked about our emotions and most of us felt fear at first.

Amani, a team member, has given us a lot to consider. She has exceptional talent in art and writing. She expressed her fear in this picture below. When I look at it, I can see she was scared, but she was also anxious and bored and even annoyed. All these emotions told me something about her. But it also told me how I was feeling. As I looked at the picture, I saw some of the same emotions inside me.

Once you examine the picture, then look at the poem Amani wrote. When you read it, you see she named it I CAN'T BREATHE. When I read it, I felt like I knew what she was saying because once again, I felt some of those feelings. Read it out loud to get the most out of her words. And every time she says, JUST BREATHE, take a breath and say those two words a little louder than the other words. It's a powerful poem.

By Amani

I Can't Breathe

Written on May 20th, 2020, prior to the death of George Floyd

Heart thumping, mind is racing and legs are shaking....Just Breathe

Lives are slipping away, families crying every day....Just Breathe

No essentials, people hoarding, forget thy neighbors ....Just Breathe

Roads are silent, stores are empty, the world is silent....Just Breathe

Daughter's pregnant, baby's coming, dad is dying....Just Breathe

Honey I'm sorry- kiss the kids, tell them I love them....Just Breathe

You're a senior now you did it, no prom or graduation ....

Just Breathe

People blame me, Coronavirus came from China....

I was just born there....Just Breathe

Social Distance, can't hug my best friends and family....Just Breathe

My classroom, now a lonely room, can't

pass a note or raise my hand,

you tell me that you understand....Just Breathe

but I can't!

This is a picture of how Julia felt when having fear. Can you see how she represented fear? Think about how you would draw your fear.

Samantha's artwork shows how she mixes fear and hope.

Look at Samantha's picture of the rainbow and then read Elif's story. Samantha tells her story through art. Elif talks about her rainbow of emotions and how she changed her outlook, letting go of fear, during the pandemic. Elif tells her through words. Do they give you the same message? Or how are they different?

The Spectrum of Life
By Elif Ak

I always like to explain my feelings with similes, because the thought process inside my head gets too chaotic and too complicated sometimes for people to understand.

I googled the word "spectrum". Google defines the word spectrum as a form of a condition that is not limited to a specific set of values but can vary, without steps, across a continuum. There it was! The perfect word to define and explain this stage of my life! I wanted to talk about the era of the pandemic in words that did not have negative connotations. For example , "a glitch", "darkness" "fearful" "uncertainty" those were the words that were felt in the back of my mind every single day of 2020 and 2021. Yet, google goes on to explain the word spectrum a little more in depth.

"Spectrum" was first used scientifically in optics to describe the rainbow of colors in visible light after passing through a prism. This is where we are, we are in the prism that awaits to see all the rainbow colors after we pass through it. (Look at Samantha's artwork and see those beautiful rainbow colors.)

This stage of my life has taught me so much more as I go back and reflect. It has taught me the value of patience, self-care and connectivity. As the world shut down, isolated humans and broke connectivity, people turned into different outlets to find happiness, fill time, and focus on what mattered. This past year was a year of growth because even though it was filled with making time for things that mattered, people lost their social interactions, a place to go to every morning, a place to dress up when they go to see their friends. Mental illnesses increased, suicide rates increased, everyone struggled. How have I dealt with this fear? I've learned to take my life one day at a time.

Naturally, among my peers and colleagues, since I am a Freshman now in college, academics occupy most of my time and in normal times we cope with it by socialization. When this coping mechanism was taken away from me, I didn't know what to do. Nobody, no human from any age group, was mentally prepared for a pandemic. My family struggled, my brother struggled, my friends struggled, I struggled. Every single day taught me a new way to face my fear with an optimistic mindset. I stopped questioning the situation of the world and started to accept it. Was it fair? No. But is anything really fair in the world?

As I learned not to question the situation of my mental state but accept it, learn and dismiss the negative thoughts, I started to be happier. I decided to work on what I wanted, to create some sort of an awareness in the world with an issue that everyone I knew was facing, every single day. I learned to take care of my mental health through various ways: making time to call relatives, friends, exercising, reading, painting, taking care of plants, baking, and getting certified with various free online platforms. I learned how to educate myself, by myself. I've learned that my own education was also another spectrum that showed me the rainbow beyond the prism every single day. I started finding the motivation to get out of bed every morning, putting colorful clothes on, my mascara on to just be at home. I knew that at the end of the day, I would always have a rainbow to reflect on and I was so aware of my own power within me and was proud of myself every single day.

Perspectives matter, as we shift our perspectives as individuals into the way we want to live our lives, our lives change complete-ly. I had a lot of dark, grey days when I just couldn't stop crying, only wanted to sleep all day, nobody answering my FaceTime calls, parents too busy doing DoorDash because they lost their jobs dur-ing the pandemic, I just couldn't see the rainbow...or the idea of a rainbow seemed so far, so unrealistic, so beyond the world's reality. Some days were so much better than others. I stopped having ex-pectations, and when you lower your expectations, you risk your discipline as well. I had to have discipline, motivation and thirst for education to get up every morning and open up my laptop at 8:10AM and shut it down briefly around 5:20PM, just to start it back up around 7:30PM to get back to homework. There was a huge disconnect. I felt an isolation and the feeling of loneliness in that 2 hours and 10 minutes of alone time off from zoom, when nobody was talking to me. I learned to accept that quietness, to understand it, to become aware of it and eventually to solve it one day at a time. Walking my dog helped, swimming helped, reading helped, asking my mom how her day was helped. After dinner, I kept busy with schoolwork, even though I dreaded it.

The generation of young students who experienced the pandemic in their college year has been damaged by the isolation of our time. We've also grown into our most powerful self by facing these mental challenges. In a chaotic world where it seemed that being on social media where we were exposed to all the chaos that was going on in the world, our young minds were filled with disorganization, uncertainty and discomfort. As I learned from many readings, from many different professors, I became more and more passionate to learn things in depth. Knowledge is another huge part of this spectrum.

I sincerely hope that everyone gets to experience the awakening that I've had during one of my recent visits to a coffee shop.

A sign read, "Every time, only once."

We only get to choose the driving forces of our lives in every situation, only once. Our lives are composed of momentary decisions we make every single day and I choose to see the rainbow beyond the prism. I hope everyone sees the rainbow beyond the prism in this crazy spectrum of life.

I reflect on my thoughts and my experiences nearly everyday. I did not want to be a cliche candidate by straightforwardly telling the reader that this past year was the most challenging year of my lifetime. But I just said it. The spectrum of life in the past year has brought me to who I am today, and I am forever grateful for the mental strength and emotional power I had to take life one day at a time.

Last year, I told my story about what it meant to be an international student and how much passion I had for the inclusion of all the colors in the world. This year, I will tell you my story of how I dealt with my own fear, how I chose courage, bravery and determination that made me realize the parallel between a spectrum of life and the power of connectivity. Because every time, only once is a way to see the rainbow beyond the prism in the spectrum of life. Here's my artwork with fear as the strongest emotion.

YOUR TURN!
DRAW YOUR PICTURE OF FEAR!

Chapter Three - **Anger**

Artwork by Cassandra

Everyone Shut Up! I Am Angry
I hate this...
I hate that ...
This is stupid dumb...

So the fear finally got less. And I understand more about what was making so many people anxious. But now I am filled with anger! It's April and I am angry at everyone. Really just mad! Nothing was normal.

Artwork by Samantha

I was working out in my room around 10:00pm when I heard a howling sound from the kitchen, yelling from the living room and I shouted to everyone to be quiet. They just got louder and louder. My head was pounding from all the noise. Pounding so hard that someone could probably hear it if they just walked by our street.

Artwork by Cassandra

    I took one step down the stairs and heard a foreign voice shouting at my dog Rosie and my Dad screaming back at the foreign voice, "Get out of here!" Then I walked down a couple more steps just to see my other dog, Chip tearing up the house. He was ripping the couch, tearing the curtains, and eating the pillows - feathers everywhere. It looked like a tornado came through our house. It was beyond anything I had ever seen, feathers everywhere. The curtains were torn apart. Scared for what was happening I tried to stop Chip who started attacking me and so did Rosie for no reason. They were enraged and I turned around and screamed for help. I pointed at the freaky villain who entered my house. "What are you doing? This is crazy. Who are you anyhow? Do I know you? You are making my house a wreck." And for my dogs to bark at me simultaneously is bizarre. I felt like I was in another world. Everyone was attacking me. I started to get angrier than I had ever been because I knew I did nothing wrong. So I scream GET OUT OF HERE. Rosie and Chip would not calm down. Just to make matters worse the foreign voice of the freaky villain started getting even louder and my head was pounding. Then all of sudden the voice started getting closer and the screaming got louder. I see this foreign voice turn into a real human and then everything goes black.

Artwork by Cassandra

I woke up covered with sweat. I realized I was having a night-mare... anger, rage, annoyed, and definitely irritated. I was angry. So much had been taken away from all of us; nobody deserves this. I was too angry to know how to deal with it.

How do we deal with our anger? Talking with friends, and trying to understand how we cope can be helpful. Anger is complicated. Let me share some thoughts with you. My anger was all over the place.

Anger is something I began to feel when everything was taken away from me. It wasn't fair. Before I could cope with it, I had to know what was making me angry. As I look back to the start of this virus, I felt anger when my parents started to make a schedule. Therefore I argued back because I did want a schedule and I was sure that all of my friends were going to basically have a break while I had to still be doing work for weeks not to mention the endless housework my mom wanted me to do. I had been angry when soccer, my gym, even school got cancelled and I couldn't do the things I love and see the people I enjoy seeing every day.

I was angry when I couldn't get near people on the Minuteman trail; when we had to self-quarantine; when we were isolated. Then the anger got worse. I started to take it out on my family but realized that it would just make the situation worse. I have pushed myself out of this anger, a little bit each day, by trying to understand why it was coming on like it did. I have had to deal with it. I started by becoming aware of what I do physically when I get angry. I narrow my eyes and clench my jaw. My family knows it right away...Noah's mad!!! Then I got into this crazy language. *"This is crazy. Why are you making me do this?"* If I am being totally honest, I blame my parents. That's normal I think. They will be there for you even if you blame them. But the anger isn't good. I finally did the body scan too, the one that helped me with my fear. It helped to calm my anger.

I also noticed that when I had a routine, I didn't get angry as often. I know my Mom tried to make me get into a routine, and I know that really does help. But it doesn't come easily. Especially when you aren't in school. Or at sports. I keep working on getting into a routine. Planning your routine gives you motivation. Don't just let your parents make the plan for you. Think about what will make you feel good and add that to your routine. You might want to try learning something new. Writing this book is new for me. I would never have had the time to do it if I was doing my old routine. So my routine now includes doing a one-hour exercise program, reading for ½ hour a day, doing school work, and writing this book with Nana for an hour. I include times to do it in this routine too. So I can check off what I did and what I didn't do.

Even with routines and body scans, I admit I still get angry at times. I have to work on my anger. I still get angry at my brothers. I still get angry at my parents. But not as often. The more I know about my anger, and the more activities and routine I have, the better I feel.

Anger is an emotion that is as basic as anxiety, fear, sadness and happiness. We all feel anger at times. We are human and when we can't get what we want, anger becomes a way we think can help us. It usually doesn't. Sometimes you can use anger in a positive way. For example, it can motivate you to succeed at a task. It's the force that drives you to do it. If you're angry at the teacher and blame her for your bad test grades, you can use the anger to motivate you to succeed. You could say to yourself, "I am not going to let anyone ruin my future!" So the anger at your teacher motivated you to do better.

During this virus it is easy to get angry because life is different for us and we aren't doing what we want to do. Human beings don't like change and COVID 19 brought about a lot of change. It made all of us change our ways.

When I think about my anger, I got angry when school was cancelled and I couldn't see my friends. My friends were angry too. Our parents were angry when they couldn't go into a coffee shop and get their coffee fix. The problem with anger during the virus is that so many people were having so much taken away that many were angry. Some didn't even realize their anger. Others felt more hostile and aggressive.

But I got really angry when my soccer was taken from me. I have said that soccer is quite important to me, but it's more than just important. Let me say that I have choices. I can adjust to "no soccer" or I can fight it. I am attached to soccer, and to my team too. When something is taken away from you that you love and really enjoy, your natural human reaction is anger. And that's what happened.

How did others deal with their anger during this COVID 19 crisis? Here again I turn to the Survey where there are some of the comments made by teenagers and adults. These were the ones that I felt were most useful.

COMMENTS ON ANGER

- "My life changed and not the way I would have wanted to" – 16 year old student

- "The fact that I can't be active" - 17 year old student

- "Feeling like I'm wasting some of the best years of my life." - 18 year old student

- "People are not being responsible in doing their part in staying in doors. It is causing a major spread in our environment. Due to this spread, I am not allowed to be outdoors or stay in my apartment in Austin, Texas. I am very active outside, so this is a challenge for me to stay inside." – 21 year old student

- "The lack of preparedness for coronavirus, and how we will be able to come out of this stronger and change the economic system. I also feel sad/angry due to the tough situations that so many people around the world are being faced with." - 29 year old employee

Look at the graph below and you can see that not too many people felt anger. Just 27.8% had a lot of anger. 50.8% had just a little anger. But still, there were some of us who felt anger. I sure did. I think teenagers get angry when they can't see their friends. I got angry when I couldn't play soccer. And when I couldn't do what I wanted to do. Teenagers want to socialize. We couldn't. And we socialize on the soccer field and in school.

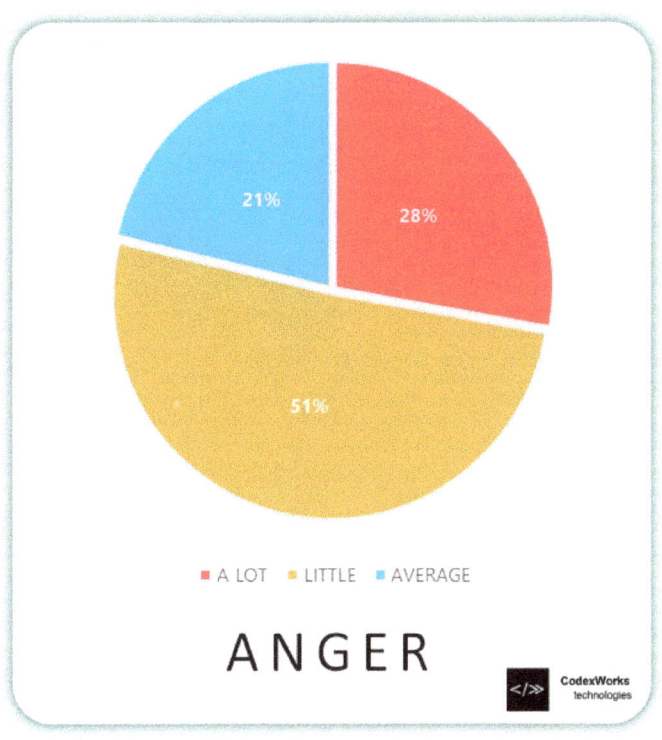

Artwork by Cassandra

Understanding Why You Are Angry

Accept that you have anger. We all do. Something's going to make you angry. You know I got angry when all that stuff was taken away from me.

"YOUR CHALLENGE"
FROM ANGER TO A SENSE OF
PEACEFULNESS

1. Find things to do that make you happy and have fun.

2. Don't focus on the negative too much.

3. Distract yourself.

4. Better understand what is happening. Ask your parents to explain the important news to you.

5. Don't watch too much news.

6. Do stuff that you enjoy.

7. Recognize that this isn't going to last forever.

8. Exercise, or play a sport either indoors or outside if it is safe out there without people.

9. Draw a picture.

10. Think about what peacefulness means to you.

Think about how you deal with anger, and write it down.

I get angry when....

_____

_____

_____

_____

_____

The first time I got angry during the coronavirus was when...

_____

_____

_____

_____

_____

How I deal with my anger....

_____

_____

_____

_____

_____

My Nana's Ideas When You Want Everyone To "Shut Up" Because You Are Angry!

When I get angry, I am sometimes not sure what is going to help me calm down. I talked with my Nana about these feelings and she gave us some tips. She believes that you can change your thoughts. If you start to recognize what you are thinking, you can then say to yourself that you don't have to think those thoughts. Each of us can figure out the best way to do this. Here's Nana's thoughts.

Finding A Positive Response

Think about why you are angry. Describe your anger. You can either write it in words, pictures, however you choose. Then try the following:

Is there anything you can think about to make you feel more peaceful? Anything you can do at the moment?

_____
_____
_____
_____
_____

Write down your thoughts when you are angry. Look them over when you settle down and you are no longer angry. What do you learn about yourself?

We all have things that trigger us - get us angry. It may be the way someone talks to you, or the way someone makes demands on you. It is something within you - that you want more freedom and you aren't getting what you want. Or you want to be left alone and you have to be with your family all of the time now. Or that you miss school and hate doing your homework alone in your room.

Something is happening within you. Figure it out. Then, you can deal with it. What makes you feel angry? What makes you feel peaceful? Go do something that feels good when you are angry, even if it takes motivation on your part. You will feel better in the end.

My Nana said, "I believe that people who feel good about themselves are kinder to others than those who don't feel good about themselves. So if you are angry, is there something you can do that makes you feel good about yourself? When people do something for others, it makes them feel good. Try to do an act of kindness for someone else and see how it makes you feel. Think of your strengths, those positive strengths you have, and focus on them. Whatever it takes, it is within you to control."

Emotions In Facial Expressions...

This may not sound like it has to do with anger, but read on. Because it does. Our faces show emotions but more often than not, we don't know what others are really feeling. If you are angry, you may frown. If you are happy, you may smile. But sometimes you don't show how you are really feeling. Nana and I created the activity on the next couple pages so you can think about facial expressions. Look at the pictures of the team members of 6 Feet Apart, starting on the next page. Guess what they are feeling as you look at their picture. Place a word that you think describes a team member based on their picture. We have listed nine words. (You can use the same word more than once.)

- Sociable
- Generous
- Funny
- Creative
- Reliable

- Hospitable
- Hard working
- Outgoing
- Unconventional
- Angry

Check your answers below and see how the team members thought about their own facial expressions. Did you guess right?

You automatically form opinions from people's facial expressions but don't assume you know how they feel. Reading people's faces is difficult. Facial expressions are a form of nonverbal behavior and when you are aware that you don't know how someone feels, you can communicate better with them than if you assume you know how they are feeling.

NOAH

EDIE

CASSANDRA

ASIA RAE

SAMANTHA

AMANI

JULIA

ELIF

Our Answers

Noah: Hard working and creative

Edie: Funny

Cassandra: Sociable

Asia Rae: Happy

Samantha: Creative

Amani: Hard working

Julia: Nonconventional

Elif: Sociable

Nathan's Picture of Anger

Artwork by Cassandra

Thank you again to Nathan Schwartz for giving us this dramatic picture of anger. As Nathan's picture shows, anger can be a difficult emotion to control. Sometimes it is helpful to do something like one of the activities you just did, or you can draw a picture. Nathan drew this picture of anger. It's fun to look at because it is so colorful yet to him he says it shows anger. When you look at this picture, what do you think of? Give it a title. Describe it with emotions.

YOUR TURN!
DRAW YOUR PICTURE OF
ANGER! OR DRAW YOUR PICTURE
OF PEACE!

Chapter Four - **Sadness**

Artwork by Cassandra

Sadness Is Spreading Like The Coronavirus

The anger doesn't last forever. It comes and goes, but when I can't see my friends and I can't do my routine, and I can't do the things I love, I start to miss them more and more. I sometimes feel just sad. It's like sadness starts to spread like the coronavirus. If the virus seems contained and getting better, I get less sad. Then when the virus reappears, so does sadness.

Artwork by Samantha

Sadness can make me feel tired and bored and make me really think about my life, my feelings and the people around me. It can make me think about everything. It even affects my dreams. Think about whether this happens to you. I bet it does.

When I am sad, I see sadness in others. It seems to be spreading everywhere. The other day I was walking the dogs and saw another family with two kids and all of them were wearing face masks. I could see the sadness in the parents' eyes. Sometimes I think I see it in my Mom's eyes. Sadness is really spreading like the virus.

Artwork by Edie

It's now late April, a month later and again the news was on. I looked at the number of cases on the bottom right corner of the TV and it showed all the cases everywhere around the world. I see the same reporter that I saw last month and she looks sad with a worried look over her face. Her bottom lip is jutted out and her eyes are almost watery. A month earlier her face expressed fear. Her eyes were wide open and her shoulders were narrowed. Now she looks sad.

I am finding sadness everywhere these days. Sadness is an interesting emotion. As I was thinking about how to write this chapter, and how to really describe to you how I felt the virus and sadness were spreading, I looked at the cover of the book and wondered how it would look if we cut it into pieces. I asked Samantha if she would be willing to do that, and she said yes. So look at the picture below. It's so different from the picture on the cover, yet it is the same drawing. In this picture, I see the virus spreading. In my mind, I want to make more little boxes as sadness continues to spread. I started feeling that as the virus spreads so does sadness. Her imaginative artwork shows you this image. Samantha wanted to show you how she can transpose a picture into a different way of thinking. In this picture, I see sadness. Each of the little boxes represent how the virus is spreading. I wanted to take the picture and add more boxes to it to show how each day and week and then month people around me were feeling more sadness. How do you see this picture? Look at the cover and you can read what Samantha said it represents. Then look at these boxes.

Samantha's words focus on her painting. "I feel as though sadness is a complicated yet necessary emotion. While we do not enjoy being sad, sadness can bring about joy and connection to others who also share the same sadness. That is why sadness in many ways represents the coronavirus. We are all dealing with the same problem and by feeling sad we open our hearts and minds to each other and form a connection that leads us on the road to happiness."

By my third week at home, I wasn't feeling happy. I know Samantha said when we feel sad we open our hearts, but that may take time. These were my thoughts. COVID is getting harder and harder. I can't get used to being in the house. I have been here for over three weeks. I am just sitting in my bedroom. I can describe my bedroom in detail with my eyes shut. I know every piece of furniture, every book and every article everywhere!!!! The walls are tan, and I have my bed in the corner. I have clothes in a white drawer right across from my bed. There are two posters on the wall: One is Ronaldo, the soccer player. He is super skilled, so fast, his foot work is incredible and I like watching him play. The next poster is when the Patriots won the super bowl. Obviously, I am a Patriots fan. Right next to my bed is a bed stand where I put my phone and my water bottle. I have a blue bean bag which sits to the right of my bed. I have all kinds of books lying around. I'm not messy and I'm not the neatest. The two things that stay the same and don't change are the two big windows for me to look out. And it's empty. No one is out there.

Artwork by Cassandra

Cassandra drew this picture because I described my room to her. She got it exactly right. I feel lonely and sad when I look outside. Sadness is also inside my house - here in front me. It is appearing with my brothers. They aren't happy. It's on social media. Everyone talks about how isolated they feel. It's on the TV. Over and over again, they say the same thing. I am sad and this virus is making many people feel sad. I think it is more than sadness though.

It was more than just missing soccer. At first, I wasn't so sad or angry, it was a shock. But it didn't hit me cause I had been playing. But as time went on, and I wasn't able to play, it kept affecting me more and more.

It's like when you have a routine and you break it, it may not throw you off at first, but then your body starts missing it. It really throws you off. It's like an addiction. I was used to playing soccer. It served me well. Then it was gone. I wanted it back. What could I do about it?

Boom!! It hits me! If I use positive emotions to get rid of the negative ones it might make me feel better and everyone else around me might be happier too. I am not going to make the virus go away. And I can't change the rules so that we all go and play soccer. It's not going to happen that way! My emotions about it are sadness though. So what can I do? Do my negative emotions cause more sadness?

I think so. Negative emotions cause more and more sadness. They even cause some people to rebel. For example, many of us get frustrated because we can't do what we want. Some of us can stay calm and get into other things. But some rebel. They rebel because they want to make their situation better. For everybody right now, it is especially difficult because it is hard to find the good in what is happening.

Artwork by Cassandra

Cassandra drew this picture showing how we can be six feet apart, but we can still find connections with one another. I remember at first when my parents said we must stay six feet apart from people in the streets - and I had to stay six feet apart from my friends. My friends didn't believe anything could happen to us and I didn't believe that either. We rebelled by hanging out together and not doing what the government recommended which was social distancing. Or what our parents told us to do. A group of us went to our school and walked around, played football, and tried not to get close to each other but we really didn't follow the rules. We rebelled, not cause we aren't good kids, cause we are, but so many negative emotions came over us.

Once the virus really started spreading in my area, I realized the danger we were causing. Rebelling made it worse and lasted longer. I tried so hard to keep my distance when I went outside.

Rebelling can cause people to do stuff that they should not do, such as not social distancing which causes the virus to spread. It is almost like a loop that's never ending. One thing affects the other. Then the other affects the other. Like, people not distancing themselves to help prevent the virus, then the numbers of people with the virus go up and people get more stressed out. So when they are more stressed out, they social distance less. And the cycle goes on and on.

But was it only me? Once again, I think about my emotions and my Survey. People felt fear just like me. And anger and anxiety too. What about sadness? So I looked at the Survey several times a day to see what was happening. Wow!!! As we were stuck in our house, more and more people were starting to feel sad. Really sad. It was spreading like the virus was spreading.

It's obvious why so many people felt sad during the virus. Sad is the expression characterized by sorrow. You are not happy. You are feeling grief, or just feeling unhappy. You aren't fulfilled. Life is not going the way you hoped. Something has made you feel not good. Sadness was an overwhelming feeling during the virus. But what happened with sadness is that it spread. We were feeling so much loss and we had nothing we could do to feel better. We couldn't play ball with our friends. Life was so different and we didn't ask for it.

Let's look at these responses to the question on the Survey: "What makes you feel sad during this virus?" So many people are feeling sad for the same reasons I was. This has never happened before, I don't think. Now, everyone is experiencing the same emotions!!! I find that incredible. Our family had our Passover Seder on Zoom, just like the 15 year old student from The United States had to celebrate Orthodox Easter over live stream. I worried about so many people dying - and so did other people. I was frustrated that my plans were cancelled, that I couldn't see my grandparents, and that I didn't want my grandparents to get the virus. These quotes below are from people in 18 countries. And we all felt the same. It still amazes me!

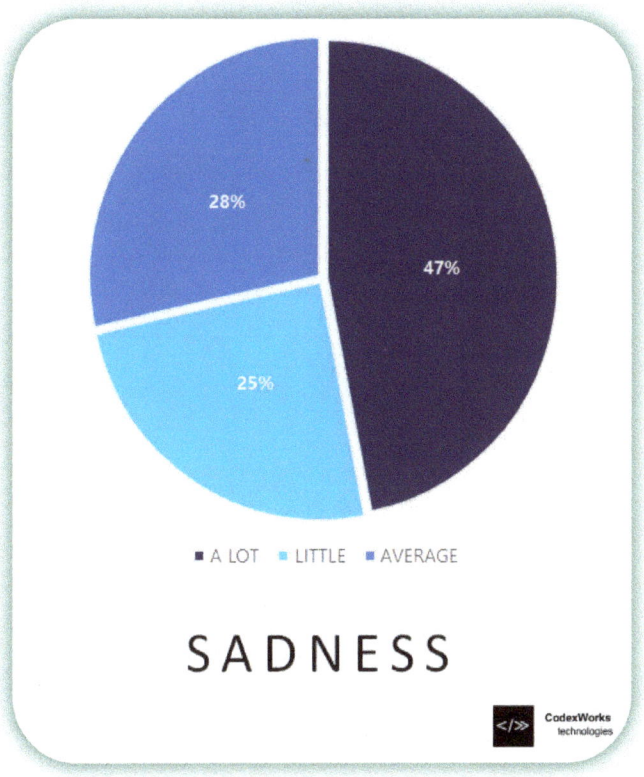

SADNESS

COMMENTS ON SADNESS

- "My orthodox Easter has to be celebrated over live stream, My freshman year which I loved ended, and I couldn't experience my 1st year of track for school." - 15 year old student

- "People dying, being far away from friends and family" - 20 year old student

- "I am worried the health and wellbeing of my more vulnerable loved ones" - 23 year old Health Care Worker

- "I am missing a lot of family events, travel with friends, etc., and I feel lonely not being able to see my loved ones/friends/coworkers during the quarantine." - 26 year old

- "Because millions of people can die" - 12 year old student

- "Less time to spend with people I care about" - 14 year old student

- "Lack of liberty and missing those dear to me" - 16 year old student

- "That all my plans were cancelled by this pandemic" - 17 year old student

I Asked Myself...

"WHY AM I SAD?" I continued thinking as I sat in my room - why am I sad? That question just kept coming to me. Over and over again. I keep thinking how so many people are sad just like me. But that doesn't help me. I go over in my head all that I miss. I think about hanging out with my friends. I want to walk into town. I want to play soccer. And I really miss the gym. But none of that helps. It's such negative energy. If I eliminate the negative emotion, I am going to be a better person and I am not going to want to rebel. When people do not rebel, they do the right thing and social distance and listen to what's best. They make the best out of what it is.

You feel better and are more productive when you are happy and positive. More productivity can lead to so many benefits, not just to you but even other people and the economy. Especially during this time when productivity is crucial because the economy is not the best. I know positive thinking is helpful. But first, I wanted to know if my brothers felt the same as I did. The Survey was proof, but what about my family? My Dad was on a work call so I couldn't ask him. My mom was somewhere in the house and not available either. So I asked my brothers. Here's their response. Remember, Zach is 12 and Liam is 8.

An Interview With My Brothers, Zach (age 12) Liam (age 8) on Sadness

1. Why are you sad?

Zach: Not seeing friends is really hard and not playing basketball in my league is just as hard. I hate it.

Liam: Scared and anxious that I would get this virus. And sad. I can't see Eli.

2. Tell me more about why you are sad.

Zach: Because if more vulnerable people got it, it could affect them and kill them. You know people who have some sickness now. And I can't see friends and that makes me sad. Kids are supposed to be with their friends. This isn't normal.

Liam: I can't play basketball and go to school and see my friends. I am sad.

3. What makes you feel not sad during this time?

Zach: Video games and playing basketball. I am getting good at both! But then Mom and Dad make me limit my video games. That gets me angry and sad.

Liam: No school, face timing friends, playing games on my phone. And magic. I am getting to be a magician and I love magic tricks. Dad teaches me because he was a magician when he was my age. They called him Magic Dan. I am Liam, the Magician.

4. Do you feel isolated?

Zach: Yes! From all the stuff I used to do, not being able to hang out with friends, I even miss Hebrew school! I never thought I would say that!

Liam: I miss my friends and doing the normal day activities. But I do magic now.

5. Do you feel lonely? In what way?

Zach: Yes, not seeing friends. That's the hardest. I keep saying that, but that's what I miss most.

Liam: Just missing my old life. I want it back.

6. What do you miss most out of your old life?

Zach: Going to different places and seeing different cultures. I miss the outside world!

Liam: Hanging out with my friends. I miss all of them.

7. What do you hate most now?

Zach: Not doing my daily routine. That's most important. I am 12 years old.

Liam: Not doing stuff like sports, school, seeing friends, going into town. We walked into downtown Lexington and got ice cream. We can't even do that anymore.

8. What do you wish will happen?

Zach: For it to go away! For it to be back to normal times. For me to walk to school and hang out with my friends.

Liam: For it to go away and do what I used to do. I keep saying the same thing over and over! I miss what I used to do.

As I heard my brothers' story, I remembered that Edie, our Team leader, had thoughts about sadness during COVID. She wanted to express them to all of you so you can see that life goes on in different ways for all of us. When something happens during COVID that is hard to deal with, COVID makes it even harder. Thank you Edie for being so honest with your thoughts.

On Sadness and Sickness
By Edie

Throughout this unprecedented time, many of the public, media, and our personal attention have been purely focused on COVID-19, and staying healthy and social distancing; however due to a recent experience of mine, I believe that it is important to acknowledge, shed light on, and show support for those who are battling a non COVID related illness or have a family member or close friend or relative battling a non COVID related illness during these times. My grandmother was diagnosed with a cancerous brain tumor and had to undergo surgery all while we are still in "lockdown" and having to abide by strict COVID related rules and regulations. Although everyone's experience is different, in my case, the process of my grandmother's diagnosis, treatment, and rehabilitation have looked very different then they typically would. For example, in the hospital, there is only one visitor per day, and the designated visitor is not allowed to come back in if they leave the hospital. These strict new rules and regulations can be frustrating and upsetting, because you are not able to be there and support your loved one in the capacity you want to. It may also feel conflicting, because even though you want to be there for a loved one as much as possible, you want to keep their best interest in mind, and limit any exposure to sickness as much as possible. It is disheartening to me that my family and I have not gotten to visit my great aunt in her nursing home, but I know that it is in her best interest and will benefit her in the long run if we do not go visit, and she and the nursing home are kept healthy ! All in all, I believe it is important for all those who have seen the effects of COVID 19 through the eyes of personal illness or a loved one's illness to know that they are not alone. Though the pandemic has made devastating situations harder, and added another complicated layer to extenuating circumstances, know that this is not the end. Continue to adapt, continue to learn, continue to be open and honest with loved ones, and do what is best for you and for your family and continue to show support for those around you, because we are growing stronger together.

"YOUR CHALLENGE"
SPREADING... OPTIMISM

My challenge has been to stop thinking the negative thoughts and try to find optimism in this situation. This isn't easy. Negative thoughts and saying negative things seem easier. But it doesn't help the situation. I made up this list thinking carefully what I would commit to do to change my feelings of sadness. Of course, sometimes you are going to be sad. Like when the virus first hit, you had to be sad. You can't pretend it is okay. It isn't. But to stay that way isn't helpful. So when you have had enough sadness, try these challenges. They may not all work for you, but maybe some will.

1. Notice how sadness appears to you - physically.

2. Talk to a friend.

3. Think about whether you are getting enough sleep.

4. Stay away from too much news.

5. Help someone else.

6. Call a friend and ask how they are.

7. Listen to music, go for a walk, read a book.

8. Tackle one problem. Start with a small one.

9. Make a To -Do list and stick to it.

10. Know it's okay for you to be sad.

Understanding Why You Are Sad...

So you are sad. So am I. Edie is sad based on her family's experience. I was sad for a long period of time. Then it goes away and sometimes it comes back. What about you?

How sad am I right now...

_____

_____

_____

_____

_____

What is making me sad...

_____

_____

_____

_____

_____

How do I deal with sadness...

_____

_____

_____

_____

_____

My Nana's Ideas... Spreading Optimism

Sit still and think about the following thoughts. Take three deep breaths. Whenever you think negative thoughts, remind yourself that you can change those thoughts. Think of optimistic things that make you grateful.

Look at the glass as half full... Do you look at the glass as half full or half empty? When things don't happen the way you want them to, it is an opportunity to discover something better than what you wanted.

Keep a journal. If you write down your thoughts, it helps you understand what you are feeling. Once you understand why you are feeling that way, you can decide whether you want to change.

I, Noah's Nana, find that optimism spreads when you help someone else. It makes you feel good. Do a Random Act of Kindness - like calling someone in a nursing home, or calling a grandparent who is sad to be isolated. Call them and share something fun and you will make them happy and that spreads, just like the sadness spreads. Helping others is one of the best ways to find optimism. You feel good.

Think of something that you do well. Let's say you are a good story teller. Then call someone and tell them a good story. Or if you play soccer, and you are good at it, do a Zoom call and show someone younger how to play soccer, even over Zoom. Just don't throw soccer balls in the house! Play it safe. You can think outside of the box to help someone feel better. I guarantee it will give you more optimism and make you feel better.

I try to practice a random act of kindness every day. I think of one thing I can do to make someone feel good. Here is my list. What's yours?

Noah's Random Acts of Kindness

1.   Do a Random Act of Kindness once a day: Call someone who lives alone and can't get out of the house because of the virus, send an email to someone wishing them a good day and say I am thinking about them.

2.   Wear a mask.

3.   Do a task at home when it's not my turn.

4.   Pick up trash on the trail.

5.   Be kind to everyone in my family, even when I feel down.

6.   Stay six feet apart and know society is about all of us and not just "me".

7.   Say thank you more often.

8.   Be kind when I don't want to be.

9.   Make someone feel good in whatever way I can.

10.   Know that life still has good times, even when there is sadness around.

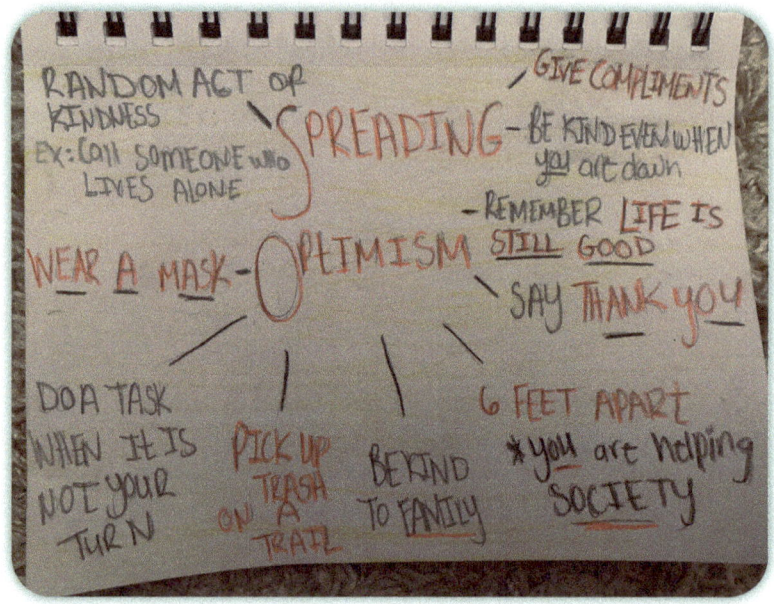

Edie really spent time on the message, how to spread optimism. It seems easy to create such a picture, but in real time, when things are so challenging, spreading optimism isn't as easy as it sounds. But if you do it, you feel good about yourself. Thanx Edie!

Pictures Representing "The Eyes Of Sadness"

Sadness was expressed differently by several members of our Team. So when you are an artist, you express your emotions in different ways. Look at the following pictures and see how Julia, Nathan and Samantha expressed sadness. I was amazed that all three pictures of the eyes expressed sadness in a different way. Look into someone's eyes when they are sad and you might see how they are feeling.

Julia

Nathan

Samantha

YOUR TURN!
DRAW YOUR PICTURE OF
SADNESS! OR DRAW YOUR
PICTURE OF OPTIMISM!

Chapter Five - **Happiness**

Artwork by Cassandra

Happiness and Hope

In this last chapter I have realized that we really are all in this together. We have experienced something that our world hasn't ever seen. We all had positive and negative emotions. We talked-about four emotions that we deal with, but this one, happiness is something that we need to have in our lives.

Artwork by Samantha

I have been writing this book for many months now and gotten to know the members of our 6 Feet Apart Team and that has been really good. I have found from them that we all want to be happy. So we have to have hope. Happiness and hope are what we need in life. Even though negative emotions mainly took over, happiness always shines, maybe just not as bright. Happiness is our safety blanket when we are filled with anger, fear, anxiety, and sadness. Happiness is not easily defined though. It has so many dimensions.

Artwork by Edie

It deals with hope and it also deals with finding meaning in our lives. Nana and I talked about happiness and how it is a different experience for each of us. So in this chapter, we have chosen to give you some insight into happiness from all of us who worked on this book together. Nana starts with her thoughts, then she interviews me and finally we have our 6 Feet Apart Team introduce their views on happiness. I found it fascinating to hear the various aspects to finding happiness within each of us. I hope you do too!

From Nana: Thank you Noah. Over the last several months, our lives have changed in a very unusual way, causing our emotions to be like a roller coaster - up and down constantly. Most people we surveyed from around the world have agreed that their emotions have been all over the place. We chose to make "Happiness" our last chapter because it takes will power and determination to find happiness during difficult times. It is also connected to hope and sometimes we just haven't felt hopeful.

"Hope" is rooted in Old English, meaning "confidence in the future." For each of us and our families, who are having difficulty with day-to-day boredom and repetitiveness of daily life, it is important to find hope. There is a saying that, "This will all come to pass." Everything changes and so will this pandemic.

It is your decision if you want to choose to be a person of hope, and personally it feels better than becoming a person of despair. Hope will allow you to live each day and recognize it as an opportunity to make your life and the lives of those around you, more enjoyable, and happier.

Happiness is a choice you can make. There are many ways to do this to make happiness a part of your daily living. You can't buy happiness with bigger and better things or travel to the far corners of the world to search for it.

If you want to find happiness, look within yourself and ask yourself an important question, "What gives my life meaning?" Right now, not in ten years, but for today. Once you know what gives you meaning, you will begin to find happiness.

Why is this question so important? If something has meaning to you, it brings on good feelings. Yes, even as a teenager, you need to be doing something that has meaning to you. Not all of the time, but sometimes.

Our 6 Feet Apart Team found meaning as they wrote this book together. Each member chose what they were going to contribute to this book based on what was meaningful to them. You now have seen their artwork, poetry, photography and music. In this chapter they express themselves by telling their stories. It has brought on happiness.

For example, Noah wanted to write a book. He wanted to write it on emotions and he found meaning in the writing. He also finds meaning in playing sports, especially soccer. If we didn't write about soccer and Noah in this book, it wouldn't tell what makes Noah truly happy. Sure, he gets happy over other things too, but soccer is so important to him. The other 6 Feet Apart Team members also find happiness in their own way. Julia loves to draw. She shows her feelings about life through her art and that gives her meaning. Asia Rae is a musician. It is her "inner calling". Had we asked Asia Rae to draw a picture, she would not have been as involved as when we asked her to create a song. And Amani sent us her bio and it flowed as though she was writing poetry. We asked her Mom, "Does Amani write poems?" "Hey, Amani," her mother called to her. "Have you ever written a poem?" Amani said no and ten minutes later, she created "I can't breathe" and handed it to her Mom. She felt those words inside of her. Edie knows what she wants to do when she goes to college. Elif is in college and she knows she loves to write but is undecided about her major. And Cassandra found meaning through active participation in the art, design and editing of this book.

If you don't know what has meaning for you, think about what you love to do. What makes you feel good? It may be hard to find because you have been cooped up in your home, with limited privacy, little contact with your friends, and less structure and routine.

To find that meaning can take time. Experiment with new ideas. Do you like to draw? Do you like to read poetry? Would you like to write it? What gets you excited? If it is gaming, what about it? If it is social interaction, with whom and about what? We all can find some things that give us meaning.

Finally, remember that everything changes and nothing ever stays the same. So have confidence in the future. Your future, the future of those you love, and the future of our world. It all begins with each one of us.

Make a commitment to bring hope and happiness into your day. This will provide you with the power to change the environment around you and then change the world for the better.

I interviewed Noah based on a Code of Happiness he and I created together. It was mid-July, 2020 when people were starting to adventure out more, yet there was still fear and confusion on how we each should live our lives. Even though Noah is a new author, a young one, his thoughts behind the scenes show what has been important to him as he wrote his story.

Nana Interviews Noah

Noah, how are you feeling now?

I am playing soccer now!!! You have no idea how happy that makes me. And I see some friends but I wear my mask. I sleep really late and my parents don't like it. I am different than when I started this book. Then, I had fear. When I reread it now, some of what I read doesn't sound like me. I am in a different place now. I have more happiness because I am seeing my friends. and playing soccer which gives meaning to my life. But now, there is talk about the virus coming back, so I am worried. I don't want to be isolated again.

What made you choose these five emotions?

We created them because we all felt comfortable with them. We could have added so many more, but these were the main ones we felt. This does not exclude others. You can even think of adding emotions if you decide to write your story.

Describe "happiness" and what it means to you.

For me, it's connecting to others. I am social so happiness is being together with other people. It's helping others, because that makes me happy. You can tell if someone is happy when they are smiling, laughing, being joyful and positive. I smile and I laugh whenever I am happy. Happiness is in the present - right now.

How would you define "hope" in your life?

Hope is what I want in the future. It is wanting a certain outcome - really wanting something to be the way you want it to be. So for me, I hope to improve as a person. That means, I improve in my soccer, in my school and in my relations with my family.

How do you find happiness in the COVID world today?

If I am productive during the day, it helps me find happiness. It makes me feel that I am getting better as a person. Every morning I think, "Will I be productive today?" I want to be and I try to be honest with myself.

What is the meaning in your life? This may change over time, but for now, what would you say?

My purpose is to be a "better me everyday." That means doing what I value most. Once again, for me, it's school, sports, family and friends.

You wrote this book and gave suggestions to others but do you listen to your own advice?

Yes, I am more aware of my feelings because I have been writing this book. My feelings have changed because I now don't feel as fearful. I learned how difficult it is to write a book on emotions. I have seen different perspectives and different backgrounds where people come from all over the world, and how not all people are the same, and yet they were experiencing the same emotions. I am aware of more than I used to be. I guess I keep growing.

Describe more about your feelings now.

Now I am happier than when I first started this book because everything is coming back. I am appreciating everything more. I don't take it for granted. I don't know how I would feel if the virus came back and we were quarantined. I wonder if I would get into the same fear. I just don't know.

What strengths have you developed while writing this book?

I definitely have improved my writing skills. That's for sure. I realized that it takes motivation and lots of effort and patience. I think I developed awareness of my strengths. I can think deeply.

How did you stay motivated while writing this book? I know there were times you didn't want to write because you wanted to be with your friends.

We came so far it would have been stupid to stop. It was an inner drive not wanting to let it go. I also know it will be meaningful to others and Nana and I had a good time doing it together.

Do you practice the meditations in this book? If so, which is your favorite?

Definitely the head to toe helps me get to sleep. That alone makes me feel better.

How have you dealt with your anger?

Kids get angry. We all do. You have to find what you enjoy and do it. I feel like that is super simple, but I believe it is true.

Do you use the techniques you offer others?

Yes, I do. Here are some of those techniques I use. If I am anxious, I think about what is causing my anxiety. I think about what I can do to make me feel better. I want to know where the emotion is coming from. Like if it is fear, why am I afraid? I do the body scan often. I distract myself when I feel anger. I find things to make me happy. I make sure I get enough sleep. So the lists I wrote, I try to follow.

Noah's final thoughts:

As I thought of all of these emotions, I have realized that each emotion brings you a feeling or a sensation and each person will experience something different. It depends on how the person perceives the emotion, physically and mentally and once they feel that, they know what emotion they are feeling. This doesn't necessarily mean that feeling is what others see.

Some people may get sad while someone else doesn't get sad over the same thing. Think about politics. You have your vote and you can vote for who you want and one side gets sad and one sad is happy depending on who wins the election. Think about sports. You watch a game and some of the people go home happy and yet, watching the same game, some go home sad. Even for some who played and won, they can go home sad because they didn't play as well as they hoped. Emotions are complicated and powerful. We have to accept them and understanding them benefits you.

If I go back to the Survey, I look at all of the emotions. Happiness is just one, an important one, but we experience them all. Look at the Survey and think about the path you took following these emotions.

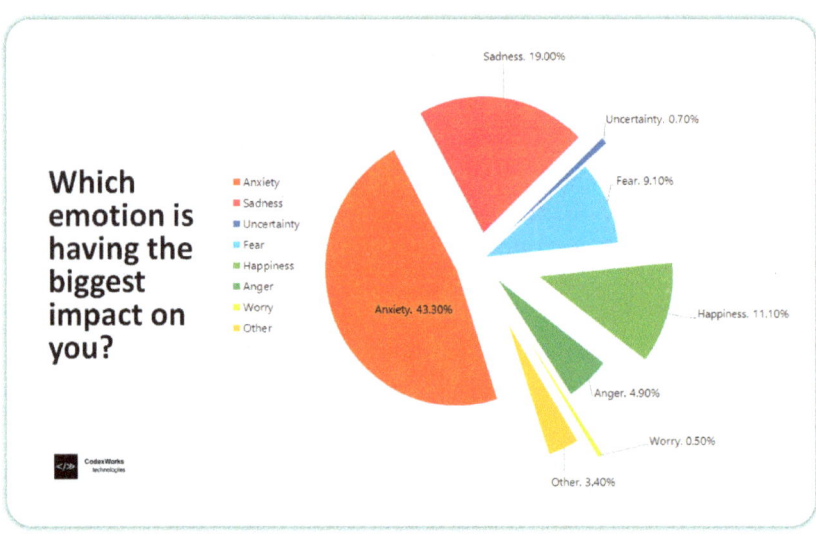

Finally Noah, one last question.
What have you learned from the 6 Feet Apart Team?

So much. They have been amazing in their team effort, their art, music, poetry, on and on. Let's start with Edie. What's happiness to you, Edie?

Edie's Story

Happiness is an extremely complex and multilayered emotion. Happiness to me is feelings of joy, feelings of contentment, feelings of excitement, and feelings of security. During these times, I realize that unfortunately it can be hard to partake in all of the things that bring you joy, or make you excited, or that make you feel secure mentally, physically and emotionally. Finding happiness right now, may feel like trying to find a ray of sun in the midst of a raging thunderstorm or catching a race horse that's gallivanting across a field that extends for miles and miles. However, through all of the change, amidst the turmoil, though it may be hidden deep down in the thick, dense underbrush of your mind and heart, I genuinely believe each and everyone of you reading this can make through these times of stress, deprivation, and uncertainty, and find happiness.

One step I believe to be important on the path to finding happiness, is to acknowledge your current negative emotion; whether that be anxiety, fear, anger, etc., and the source of that emotion. Feeling your negative emotion to full capacity gives your mind and body the freedom to let it pass. Then you feel happier, because you aren't suppressing the emotion and letting it well up inside you. You are expressing and acknowledging it. Target the source of the emotion to help you move forward into happiness.

I try to remember the quote " Lord grant me the serenity to accept the things I cannot change, courage to change the things I can, and wisdom to know the difference." This inspires me, and can hopefully remind you, to be proactive and work hard to change things that make you upset which you are able to control, and release the burden and "weight" of the things that you can't.

Every one of us releases a negative emotion in a different way. You can be talking to family or a friend, art, listening to music, watching a movie, or even just simply spending time alone and this can release negative emotions. The important thing is that you take safe and productive measures to work through your emotion, because it allows you to be more positive, and it takes your mind off your negative emotion, and possibly you will feel happier.

After you identify your emotion, and address the problem, another tool you can utilize on your path to happiness is to discover your core happiness elements. You can find them by thinking of three or four non- material simple things that make you happy.

For me personally, my core happiness elements are music, exercise, friends/family, and nature. Your personal core happiness can range from the smell of your favorite candle burning, or after-noon snuggles with your dog! Anything works! Once you are able to pinpoint a few small intangible consistent things that make you happy, when others, seemingly bigger or more important things go awry, you will be able to resort back to your core elements and they will make you feel better. The "big" things will not feel so overwhelming, or sad, or scary.

Everyone has their own happiness journey. There is no one set of steps or roadmap that everyone can follow to achieve happi-ness. Do what you have to do, to feel, acknowledge, and address or release your negative emotion. Find hobbies, passions, and simple nonmaterial things you can turn to when you are anxious, sad or angry. Although it may be draining and extremely hard to think positively, your attitude, work ethic and character will get you far. Happiness is circular, so though it may leave, it will come back around. In the meantime, it is pivotal to know you are not alone in a scary, unpleasant time, and together we will come out of this as better, kinder, more appreciative and happier people.

I find a purpose and passion in photography, because it helps to fulfill two of my four core happiness elements, nature and family. I get to spend time and encapsulate the beauty of nature, and it also helps me connect with my mom who is an art teacher. Getting to have in depth conversations about our favorite artists/photographers and composition techniques brought me lots of joy! Here are two pictures.

Photograph by Edie

I wanted to include this photograph, because it encompases two of my core happiness elements - Nature and Family. This tree is right outside my grandma's house, and brings back lots of fond memories of climbing and swinging from the branches when I was younger. I also found beauty in how the sun was shining down and making shadows and highlights on the bark. I am glad I chose to photograph the tree from this angle, because it accentuated the blue sky and natural light.

Photograph by Edie

This picture was taken at a horse farm I volunteered at the Hugh O'Brian Youth Leadership conference. Being on the farm and immersed in nature and having the experience of taking care of horses - even for one day, was an amazing experience and made me extremely happy. I am so glad I captured this moment, and it will always remind me of my time coming together with other youth leaders and getting to explore the true meaning of volunteerism and giving back to the community.

"Your Challenge"
Your Path Toward Finding Happiness Based
On Edie's Thoughts...

NAME YOUR CORE HAPPINESS ELEMENTS

1. _____

2. _____

3. _____

4. _____

WHAT IS YOUR HAPPINESS JOURNEY?

Cassandra's Story

Before I start my story about happiness, I would like to share that it is very difficult for me to write my opinion for people to see because I live in fear of people nitpicking what I said and I might unknowingly offend someone.

However here it goes so…happiness can be hard to find in a difficult time like the present with the virus going on and all the hate, but I will say once found it is the best feeling ever and I don't want to let it go. Even though happiness can be hard to find, it does not make it impossible! The feeling of joy, hope and happiness is easier than being sad. I hate being sad and overwhelmed.

When I lose happiness I try to regain it as fast as I can, kind of like a sickness. When people get sick they rest and try their very best to get healthy as soon as possible. That is me not only when I am sick but feeling down. When I am sad I get a headache and I feel so weak, so I do all I can to get back on the bright side.

Keeping your sunny side up is doing things even if you don't have the energy. Motivate yourself to do it as you will feel better afterwards. We all feel good once we accomplish something. It can be as simple as getting up to go on a walk, do the laundry, clean the house, or a hobby you like to do. Happiness to me is being able to laugh, smile, be with people I love, thinking positive, doing good deeds and not worrying. What makes me happy is being active. I love playing field hockey, watching Penn State Football, swimming, completing chores around the house, making my friends and family smile and brightening their day, and having faith in God.

Happiness feels light and feels like nothing could stop or hold me down. There is no cloud hanging over my head and I can be myself. We are the happiest when we can express our true selves. I can kind of get butterflies in my stomach if I am very excited. Happiness can be hard to find like I said in hard times but how you can find it is to be thankful for what you do have. During this virus and quarantine I am thankful for the basic but very important three things; a roof over my head, food on the table, and clothes to wear. I am also thankful that I have a phone and other electrical devices to entertain me and keep me connected with my friends. You have no idea how many times my phone will get down to 17% when I'm on FaceTime with my friend(s).

I would like to give a disclaimer before I share my advice. This is my opinion and what works for me does not work for everyone because we handle our emotions in different ways. So find the outlet that works best for you. I don't walk in your shoes so sadly I can't connect personally to you and your struggles but hopefully one of these things can help you. My advice to you in retaining happiness is...

Cassandra's 10 Tips Toward Happiness

1. **"Treat People with Kindness"**! We can lose happiness when we are rude to people and people are rude to us. If we all start learning to "Treat People with Kindness" and leading by example the world will be a happier and nicer place. We can lose happiness when we get annoyed or mad at someone for doing something we don't like. Remind yourself that you can choose how you feel and that "People are Different"- Florida Georgia Line. I see among kids in my school, people pick on and don't want to be a part of the people who act a little odd. Kids think everyone has to pass a certain "coolness test" for them to be nice and treat them normal with respect.

2. **Do things you love.** That sounds simple but if you do something you are not passionate about and you do it for someone else's sake, it may or may not benefit you. You may feel stuck and then you can't get out of it. Build confidence or find someone you trust to help you get out of it.

3. **Look at the beauty right in front of your face.** Especially if you find yourself not being happy when looking at your friends or celebrities through a screen. Don't let Social Media and jealousy take

the place of the beauty in front of your face. This is not uncommon, I fell down that hole and I was very ungrateful and miserable about my life because I was looking at others on Instagram and becoming jealous. I took a 2 week break and in that time I was able to accomplish so much. The first days were a struggle, but after those couple of days I didn't want to go back.

4. **Make the little things worthwhile because that's all you need in life.** We live in an era where you NEED to have LOADS of money and luxury items to mean something and be someone but with a great personality and by just being you, you are special!

5. **"Every day above ground is a great day. Remember that"** –Pitbull. from "Time of Our Lives" by Pitbull and Ne-Yo. Life and time is a precious gift, don't let it slip away and be wasted. Tomorrow is a whole NEW day and that is very powerful to know.

6. **Don't live in drama.** I know sometimes this is out of our control but try to walk away when drama is happening or being talked about. Don't encourage it and spread it. We also live in a time where drama is found entertaining (reality TV, school drama/gossip), but it's not healthy. It spreads negativity and tension which blocks out room for happiness and joy.

7. **Keep quiet.** Some things are not worth arguing about. When someone starts arguing with you, be calm and just let them say everything that they have to say and leave it at that. If you really need to say something, say it in a normal tone and volume. I do this when my parents get mad and when I listen to them and make them happy they will later respect and trust me more.

8. **Punch your pillow before bed to let all your frustration of the day go.** Afterwards, with the anger released you can sleep peacefully. Another plus side is you get your pillow fluffed up.

9. **Turn to your faith.** I am an Orthodox Christian and I have a very close relationship with God. God always listens and doesn't

verbalize his opinion back, yet he leads me in the best direction. If you are a person that just needs to get it off your chest and not get advice back, God is a great outlet. If not, talk to a loved one who is a good listener. Ask them politely to just listen.

10. **Doodle.** Art is not for everyone but a little doodle can be relaxing. That's what I do, I doodle and it makes me feel relaxed. Art tells its own story even if it's sloppy. When you are feeling depressed and all you can draw is something sad, DO IT! Afterwards you can release that negative emotion by ripping it up. Art allows you to escape from the world and express your emotions.

"Your Challenge"
Your Path Toward Happiness
Based On Cassandra's Suggestions

HERE'S CASSANDRA'S TIPS. CREATE YOUR OWN OR USE HER WORDS!

1. "Treat People with Kindness"!

2. Do things you love.

3. Look at the beauty right in front of your face.

4. Make the little things worthwhile because that's all you need in life.

5. "Everyday above ground is a great day. Remember that!"

6. Don't live in drama.

7. Keep quiet.

8. Punch your pillow before bed to let all your frustration of the day go.

9. Turn to your faith.

10. Doodle.

YOUR TIPS TOWARD HAPPINESS

1._____

2._____

3._____

4._____

5._____

Our next 6 Feet Apart Team member takes creativity and expression to the next level. Asia Rae Smith not only was inspired to compose music, but shares how her composition helped her overcome her own negative feelings and express her emotion.

Asia Rae's Story

Happiness to me is music. I love it and it makes me feel good. Sometimes it is hard but I would never give it up. As a musician I definitely have had many obstacles. One of the biggest obstacles was myself. There is a program for young musicians here in Pittsburgh called All City. I entered the program in 7th grade as a violinist. For my age I was a little advanced so I was given a position with the older kids. They had to have been teenagers at the time and that terrified me. I was also given a solo to play. The kids that I played with were very intimidating and much more experienced than I was which I wasn't used to. I was used to being the leader in my musical position and the fact that I wasn't anymore made me feel out of place. The kids weren't mean to me and they didn't treat me differently. I was just scared as any 7th grader would be. At the end of the program we get to perform for our parents and anyone else that wants to see the show. I tried so hard to give up my solo because I wasn't confident. Everyone kept pushing me and telling me that I was good and it would be great for me. But I wouldn't listen to them. I soon realized that I was standing in my own way. Everyone knew I could do it except for me. But I did it!!!! I performed that same song and the solo with ease! The craziest part is that that was less than a year ago and now I wouldn't think twice about performing for someone!

The crazier part is now I wrote the following song dedicated to all who are suffering from COVID 19. Included is the sheet music, but you can see me playing the song in this book and then on the piano on YouTube. I am happy when I think of how much I have accomplished.

"6 Feet Apart"
A Song Dedicated To All Who Have Suffered During This Pandemic

At first when I started to write the following piece of music I tried to take others' feelings into account. Although I quickly realized it had to be from my perspective. The beginning of the piece is very sad and somber and it represents how I felt at the start of quarantine. I didn't have anything to do which I wasn't used to having so much free time. I was used to being busy and always having something on my plate and I was lost. But as the piece progresses it develops a happier tone. That was around the time when my school started to sort things out and I started to have my usual school work. So I had a routine again. I realized that people were being treated for the virus and that people were able to leave their houses and go places. I had some normalcy and so did others. Toward the end of the piece I made it slow down a bit and that's where I am right now. Everything now is almost normal for me in the summertime. I don't feel as out of place as I did before and I feel I am back together. The song is all over the place because that's how my emotions have been. It represents how I actually feel on the inside. I did feel a bit out of place as all of us have when we are in such a chaotic situation. If any of you play the piano, try to play my song. That would make me very happy!

6 Feet apart - Emotions All Over The Place!

Asia Rae playing her song, 6 Feet Apart: Emotions All Over The Place!

Your Challenge Based On Asia Rae's Musical Suggestions

"YOUR CHALLENGE"
FINDING HAPPINESS THROUGH MUSIC

YOUR FAVORITE SONG THAT GIVES YOU HAPPINESS

YOUR FAVORITE INSTRUMENT THAT GIVES YOU HAPPINESS

YOUR FAVORITE TYPE OF MUSIC

As Cassandra, Asia Rae and Edie point out there are lots of physical things you can do to overcome your emotions. Next you will hear from Julia, who will share some of the mental characteristics and personality traits that she believed helped her to reach happiness.

Julia's Story

Happiness and hope are two things that people are able to access during different activities and experiences. For me, I believe my strengths that give me both hope and happiness are my determination to succeed in all areas of my life. Determination is something that I feel I naturally possess and am able to apply to most areas of life. I think it is one of my greatest qualities. I play soccer and basketball, which requires a lot of dedication to become a good player. I am determined to be the best player I can and with lots of practice and it shows when I compete. I consider it a success when you meet a goal you set to achieve. Determination also motivates me intrinsically because I want to prove that I can be the best I can be in whatever circumstance I face. I want to help make the world a better place. I do this by helping others whether it is raising money, donating items and volunteering my time to various organizations brings me great joy. I love seeing how my help can benefit others. I am determined to make the world a better place, especially for women.

I am inspired by different mediums within the art world, especially music. Music attributes a lot to my artistic inspirations. Sometimes it may be a lyric or a stanza that inspires me and I am able to show that inspiration through my paper and pencil. Music and art takes me to a different world. It allows me to disconnect from reality for the 4 minutes or so that the song is on and I am lost in the song and sounds it provides. This experience often can be extended into my art work. Art also provides me an outlet to escape reality.

Sometimes when you look at art it unlocks a part of you that you didn't know you had. Sometimes you may feel something emotional. I feel my artwork is powerful because it takes the viewer on a roller coaster of emotions. It can be sad, happy, nervous, excited or anxious. My art can inspire others because they are able to make personal connections with drawings. I like to leave my work unnamed so the viewer can make their own judgment about it. Some people use color to express their emotions, however I prefer to do black and white so my emotional message does not get lost.

Here's some of Julia's artwork. How do they inspire you?

Your Challenge Based On Julia's Encouraging Suggestions

"YOUR CHALLENGE"
YOUR PATH TOWARD HAPPINESS AND HOPE

WHAT ARE YOUR STRENGTHS?

WHAT WILL YOU DO TO HELP OTHERS?

WHAT DO YOU LIKE TO DO THAT BRINGS ON HAPPINESS?

Amani's Story

Covid-19 has changed life as we know it, and permanently I fear! We were all forced to put our lives on hold. We were all tossed into a slow torturous world wind, full of the unknown. We are now living a life, unaware of what comes next. This undoubtedly, has been my life's greatest test. Even in this madness, I have been able to maintain some iota of sanity by holding on to the one I love the most. I enjoy family game nights with my mom and brother, binge watch Netflix, FaceTime my friends and even eat party size bags of my favorite chocolate cookies- lol. I can't believe I just actually admitted that. I have also been able to return to volleyball practice at my high school and I'm working on mastering baked salmon. I have learned a lot about myself and perseverance. I have learned to focus on the positive in every situation. While this entire ordeal has been challenging, I have a lot to be grateful for. Myself and my family are healthy. I wake up every morning and go to bed every night knowing that I am loved. I am my brother's hero and my mom's backbone as she says often. I have true friends and hope for a bright future. I am an overcomer and I'm ok with that. Does it make me happy? I guess so!

Your Challenge Based On Amani's Moving Suggestions

"YOUR CHALLENGE"
YOUR PATH TOWARD HAPPINESS AND HOPE

WHAT ARE YOU GRATEFUL FOR?

WHAT DID YOU LEARN ABOUT YOURSELF DURING THIS VIRUS?

Sam's Story

Happiness isn't just one thing or an object to me it is a feeling that consumes me every once in a while. It is hard to write about happiness because this year has been many things and happiness is only a small contributing factor. However my happiness stems from those I am around and doing what I love and not caring what others think. One of those is art! I feel free whenever I paint and I just let the brush guide me.

On the other hand, it isn't that simple, but I wish it were. You can't always just paint your problems and sadness away. Whenever I think of happiness, I think of a challenge. I also think it is more of a journey and not a one and done. It's hard, it really is. I think the first step is loving yourself because otherwise you'll never be happy. This is something that personally I have struggled with and I still struggle with is accepting all parts of myself and embracing my flaws. There is no secret, no shortcut, it just takes time.

Happiness is definitely the emotion that frustrates me the most, it comes when you aren't looking for it and doesn't come when you are. Happiness has a lot to do with accepting who you are and accepting who you are not. Whenever I paint, I feel calm and happy in the moment, although I always end up painting or drawing something sad or with a sad connotation. So does that mean I am not truly happy, I just enjoy painting what I truly feel or am I content in drawing the sadder parts of life because there is always light in the darkness?

Besides art, it's hard to describe what makes me happy, because sometimes I am hanging out with my friends and I share a laugh or two and feel happy but then I can come home and feel like I have the whole world on my shoulders, all my insecurities overweighing on me. When this happens, and it happens a lot, I have to ask myself: "Am I truly happy or is my happiness a mask?" Most of the time it is a mask. I wake up every morning feeling sluggish and bothered, and then I spend hours getting myself to look presentable so I feel good about myself, but let me tell you, it doesn't always work because that is my mask. I had a rough start to my sophomore year for that very reason: I was not very accepting of myself because of my insecurities. It was a time of my life when I felt lost, and couldn't even find an ounce of happiness.

I was skeptical at first about writing what happiness means to me. I honestly think that a majority of the time, happiness is a mask and that there are two different kinds. There's short term happiness that happens all the time, when you're laughing with friends, or just doing something that you love, because those things don't last forever.

The other is long term happiness and that one is harder to come by. It is something that may not come until you're in your 30s or even later, sometimes it takes a lifetime. The first step is loving yourself and all your imperfections and that won't happen until after high school, and even college, because you're still growing and comparing yourself to others.

When told I was going to be writing this, I thought to myself, I could just make something up and lie to myself about happiness but I didn't want to do that. I wanted to be honest with you all. So my advice to all of you struggling to find happiness during this time is to remember to love every bit of yourself, I do this by treating myself every once in a while and complimenting myself on the daily (it doesn't make you conceited, it makes you self-aware and beautiful).

My other piece of advice is just to enjoy yourself, eat that burger, hang out with that one person, because you want to, not because you were told you can't. Listen to yourself, listen to your body and do what you need to do, because only you know what makes you happy. I challenge myself and all of you to start this process by writing down 5 things that you love about yourself (you can write about your physical appearance but keep in mind that it will be more effective to write about what's on the inside. For example: I love that I always try and help others when they need it).

"Your Challenge" Based on Samantha's Words on Happiness

5 THINGS YOU LOVE ABOUT YOURSELF

1._____

2._____

3._____

4._____

5._____

WHAT DO YOU FIND MOST CONFUSING ABOUT HAPPINESS?

DO YOU EXPERIENCE MORE LONG TERM HAPPINESS OR SHORT TERM?

Elif's Story

BRIDGES

John Ringling Causeway Sarasota, FL.

Photography by Elif

  I wanted to call my story bridges. Yes, bridges have some kind of an emotional parallel to my feelings in the past year. There is a bridge in Sarasota, my hometown. It is about 950 meters (3,097.04ft) long and 20 meters (65ft) high from the water. It is called the John Ringling Causeway. I walked on this bridge almost 4 days a week, every single week last year.

  I am only talking about this because I think it is a great way to explain how bridges can sometimes amplify the struggles we face in life. This bridge is tall and there's an incline towards the middle of it, duh it is a bridge. This incline always has an effect on my legs and they are usually sore if I walk the bridge back and forth for more than two times. I wish there was a bridge to walk in every city. I believe one's life is composed of hundreds and thousands of bridges we walk on throughout our lifetime. When my family migrated to the United States in 2012, the bridge was so long and the transition to a very unrelated country and culture shock it brought into my life still resonates with me as I enter my 20th year in my lifetime. Who would have thought that I would be writing about my past in a book about covid— 8 years later than my arrival.

My brother and I were never exposed to the English language before we came to the United States from Turkey, let alone engage in the minimal conversation, we barely knew how to say "hello". Turkish language has nothing to do with English language, and why did people have to speak so fast all the time? I was placed in an ESOL (English as a second language) class right when we got to our first public school in a town called Rockford in the state of Illinois. Due to my lack of experience with the language, I was forced to repeat my fifth grade year in elementary school because according to the state guidelines, I wasn't "capable" to be a middle school student. As I go back in time and reflect on the education I got that year, I cannot stop to think about how my ability as a student was determined by a bunch of adults that sat in chairs and talked about public schools and funding all day long. I will never be able to take that year back, maybe— just maybe if I had that year, I would have had an experience in college for a year before the pandemic, but there's no way for them to give me my year back now is there?

I was placed in a classroom with kindergartners that had foreign parents at home.

I was taken out of 5th grade level English to be in ESOL and play games designed for younger students. I felt betrayed by the education system my family came to the United States for. I was scared to feel like I wasn't capable of being a satisfactory student, I felt lonely, I felt like an outsider. Classic immigrant story, I did not fit into a bubble of students that have excellent academic standing, I was treated like a younger mind, but in reality, I just didn't know English. As I go back and remember those days, I don't feel angry anymore, I feel empty. My identity as a Turkish student created an assumption for the educators in the United States that I did not meet specific academic achievements. When I was in Turkey, I was advanced in math, art, ceramics, and Turkish literature. I went to one of the best academies in Istanbul. The way that my hard work, my late night studies, my practices from my childhood memories, my discipline as an achieving student was missing, it was unseen and uncredited due to a barrier of a language made me question the importance of my Turkish identity, my mother tongue, my cultural diversity and my ability as a learner. This was my first bridge.

A classic immigrant story parallels what we have been going through as a world in the past year made me realize how much of a mental pandemic this was as much as it is a virus.

It made me understand how much of a social dependency we, humans, needed in our daily lives. People want to be acknowledged, be credited for their successes, become academically acknowledged, people want to go out to lunches with their colleagues, people want to be able to travel safely, they want to go back to their offices, be able to see elderlies, students want school experience, we all want friends, social connections, we want to be inspired, be passionate, be productive, determined… We want our social identities and social scene back.

The past year has been both physically, mentally and socially challenging for every single human on this planet. Sometimes I cannot stop but to wonder if the United States as a developed country has struggled this much in the world, what must be like in lower developed countries? Has this always been an issue? Perspectives, power and influences on human lives have always been significantly harder to shift when it comes to helping the humans in need.

You cannot stop but to wonder, is this really what humanity is? If people like myself suffer this much in their head, then what happens to the people that do not have anything?

I cannot help but to question the concept of fairness in the world? Was it fair for me to be held back a year then miss out a year from college? Was it fair for my parents to work so hard for their degrees only for it to not count in the United States? Is it fair to the students in the northern regions of the United States to be in school virtually and miss out on experience while southern schools continued like the pandemic didn't even exist? Is it fair for the global economies to suffer greatly due to international travel bans? Is it fair for the developed countries to be vaccinated while the lower developed countries have to continue on with the suffrage of a global pandemic? Is it fair for young adults like me to have a lack of resources to be helped with my mental facilities? Is it fair to feel depressed over a global pandemic while you still have a lot of privilege over other nations in the world? Is it fair to be dependent on a simple text in your phone, maybe a notification on your instagram to feel like you are not alone? Is it fair to want to sleep all day long every single day? While suicide rates increase tremendously in the United States in the young population as babies suffer from lack of clean water in Yemen? Is anything really fair? My heart-breaks every single day, because I feel so much. This is another bridge.

This is where we embrace human emotions like fear, anxiety, sorrow, anger and frustration to overcome days that seem like the entire world is going down in flames. We as humanity are challenged with a physical, mental, economical and emotional pandemic where we just need to face human emotions and the concept of fear and spread kindness in the world.

If there was no judgement, more desire to help others, less selfishness, more cultural exchange, more curiosity, more creativity, less materialism and resources to aid humanity rather than focusing on singularity, maybe we wouldn't be this damaged and more empowered as a society during these chaotic times.

When we go back and acknowledge how the most of the problems in the world are like inclines in bridges where it seems so hard to get through, but with hope, determination, optimism, love, and more humanity, these continuous inclines might not always seem and feel so frustrating to go through in our lives.

We must have hope, we must adopt the feeling of sharing, listening, understanding and loving one another without any judgement. We will not bleed this much as a world facing these pandemics if we face our bridges and keep walking on them, one at a time.

Artwork by Elif

If we want to talk about our emotions as if they follow a pattern, spectrums and pathways, we need to know that a balance in this world is the most optimal reward.

In my artwork, I wanted to establish how much of a desire we all have for a balanced, healthy and human way of living. We all miss our normality, our daily routines and social scene and I hope to remind everyone that our balance remains within ourselves more than ever now.

Your Happiness "Challenge" Based On Elif's Words

Write down five things that you are grateful for right now, today, repeat this "challenge" tomorrow! Then think about how it feels to be grateful.

1._____

2._____

3._____

4._____

5._____

Think about one thing that you are looking forward to in the near future and what are you most excited for?

THE 6 Feet Apart Teams'
Conclusions

Now that you have heard from us, let's dive into how you can find happiness based on the information you have read within this book. Spend time doing something that you like to do and that you also are good at doing. Think about Julia. She loves to draw. She loves the emotions that come out when she creates her artwork.

Asia Rae uses music to express and feel her emotions to the fullest. She feels the music. She created the song for you to feel the emotions expressed in it. You may feel other emotions than hers, but that's okay. She feels to fullest capacity through the song she wrote. It took her a lot of time to create this song because she talked with us about how she wanted to start the song with sadness and end it with hope. She translated that into her music.

Our 6 Feet Apart Team shared our own stories so you could see, more likely than not, that we have a lot in common. Although our pieces are very different, the things we shared accomplished one common goal - to make us feel happier. Some of us feel through music. Others through art or writing or photography or poetry. It doesn't matter what you do, it's what you feel when you are doing it. That's how it works for us. And this is what we want for you too. **Bit of advice from us.** Internal and external factors make you feel the way you do. Internal ones are inside of you. External ones are outside of you. You often can't control the external ones, so work on the internal. They are yours and yours alone.

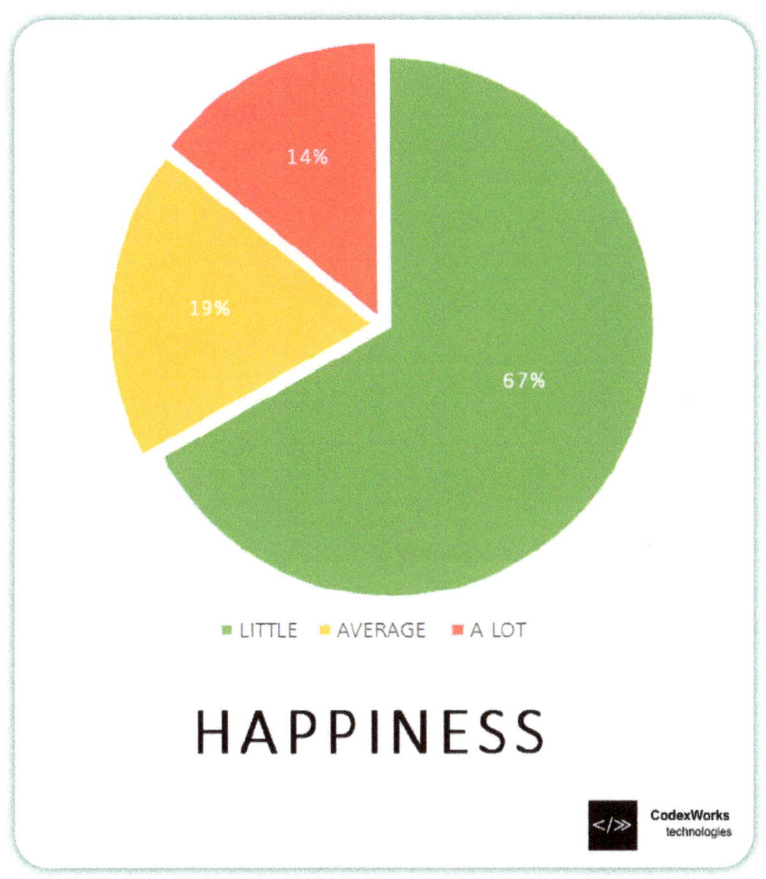

We Offer Happiness and Hope To You!

Artwork by Cassandra

Samantha's hope for the future

YOUR TURN!
DRAW YOUR PICTURE OF HAPPINESS AND HOPE!

The 6 Feet Apart
Virtual Museum
of Arts and Science

Artwork by Samantha Rosser

The 6 Feet Apart Virtual Museum of Arts and Science is created to preserve, interpret and display art, culture and scientific data for the education of all of us as teenagers about the COVID 19 pandemic. It is also a museum for teachers and parents to get the most up-to-date research on how the pandemic affects teenagers; for health professionals to include their research on trauma, and for teenagers across the globe to have their stories included along with ours.

We want the material in this book to become a historical document and conserve our stories and yours through its research and tangible art, poetry and writings. We hope to foster a deeper understanding of our views, as we share authentic stories about our generation living through this pandemic. Within this museum, we can gain critical thinking skills through the Five Emotions Survey, empathy through our personal stories, and practical steps to reduce stress during challenging times.

We believe that we can build resilience. We may not overcome all of the difficulties but we can gain skills to help us cope. We, as the 6 Feet Apart Team, hope to challenge and inspire other teenagers to discover their own path just as we have discovered more about our own.

The Rooms In The Museum

Here's what you will experience when you go online to the Virtual Museum. As you enter the museum you will be asked to take the Survey. This is the same survey that 500 people took as we were writing the book. It is based on the 5 emotions you just read about. You enter the museum and you are given a global passport. This is your travel document to explore the museum. You can go into any of the rooms. Each room has something that may be of interest to you, your family or your school educators. You can also enter with your friends. As the holder of your passport, you follow the guidelines in that room, read the information, complete the questions if you so choose, and then get a stamp on your passport that shows you have entered that room.

If you complete ten rooms or more, you become a diplomat. This gives you recognition and certification of your involvement. Your passport does not expire so you can go back to the museum whenever you wish.

Here's some of the rooms you might find in the museum.

1. How to Experience The Virtual Museum

2. 6 Ft. Apart ...The Book

3. The Mission and Vision of The Museum

4. Meet The Team: 6 Ft. Apart Team Bios and Videos

5. Meet The Codex Team: Pictures and Description

6. Meet The Mental Health Team: The Board, Susan and Sally Conversation, etc.

7. The Romanian Room

8. The Czech Room

9. The Polish Room

10. The Washington D.C. Room

11. Mindfulness and Meditation Room

12. Building Resilience: Learning Simple Skills

13. Storytelling Framework

14. The Fear Room

Exploring **6 Feet Apart**

Words From Our Coaches
Susan Shapiro
Simona Baciu
Dr. Sally A. Baas

A Unique Concept

When we read a book we most often have the expectation that the author is an adult with vast knowledge and life experience in the subject matter. What is amazing in "6 Feet Apart" is that the author is a teenager who surprises us with his mature perspective on the changes this difficult period of the COVID Pandemic brought into his life. Noah's example of perseverance and commitment to get this book written can be a good role model for all of us.

6 Feet Apart is a unique concept which addresses young people and adults globally. His self-questioning and questioning of others, and the fact that he managed to build a team of eight teenagers, who never had met except through Zoom, is refreshing to read. They all contributed their personal talents and strengths. Noah's grandmother, Susan Shapiro, a published author guided and inspired the 6 Feet Apart Team to be creative and think critically. The book is proof that we can learn from each other and that everyone's contribution matters... a universal message during a time when we are all experiencing the same crisis.

The topics addressed in 6 Feet Apart are of great interest to each of us. Emotions are part of our lives and we often take them for granted. They influence the way we think and act; they influence our daily lives and they influence our relationships. Noah and his fellow team members take courage to talk about emotions and this will surely inspire other young people to become aware of their emotions, both in difficult times and in times of joy and happiness. Other students will be emotionally fulfilled, because they will know how to approach with naturalness and normality both negative and positive emotions, embracing both aspects as a natural part of their lives.

Another important lesson we derive from this book is that teamwork can be the foundation of a successful project. Each 6 Feet Apart Team member brought positive strength, personal interest, and positive thinking. This environment helped to sustain their motivation and enthusiasm to complete this book. While reading their stories, we discover the beauty and power that lies in each of them. Learning done in this way lasts and gives us wings, when we don't feel like you have them anymore.

Imagine a class in which each student brings what they do best and contributes to the learning of others. This is the magic that this 6 Feet Apart Team created by writing this book. The learning experience of these young people can certainly be replicated as a peer education program.

The team's message is the following: no matter how old we are, we all have feelings; what we do with them, and how aware we are that they influence our lives, depends on each of us. We all go from fear to anxiety, anger, sadness and finally the happiness we are all longing to achieve. Get ready to explore "6 Feet Apart"!

Simona Baciu

Founder Transylvania College

Cluj Napoca, Romania

Co-Author The Teacher Within: A Mindful
Journey Toward Well-Being in the 21st Century

Mental Health and Belonging

6 Feet Apart has been written to document your experience as teens during COVID. But it is more than a book. It created a network between the teens who wrote the book and their coaches who are a different generation. We all belonged together on this journey, helping one another and valuing each other. All of us have been tested during COVID-19 and we all have struggled to feel mentally healthy, as we have suffered a loss of belonging.

This book is a tribute to all of us, and to you. We can connect with one another. We can belong. Think about the team in 6 Feet Apart. It has been designed, written and originated by teens your age, in the midst of this pandemic who all were developing their identity, gifts, and talents as they worked together with us as their coaches. They bonded with us, and we bonded with them and together we created a sense of belonging, even during the toughest of times. The 6 Feet Apart Team allowed us into their lives. We appreciate their openness. We learned from them and I believe they too learned from us.

It is not just during COVID that has driven all of us to think about belonging. Belonging is a part of who we are. As a Professor, past Principal, and School Psychologist, I have worked on many projects with thousands of students. I have found that belonging is a concept that is needed with people no matter their age. Belonging is part of life. But you can't just assume you belong. Research tells us in order to have well-being we need to have and practice self-awareness, self-management, social awareness, relationship skill-building and responsible decision-making. These skills have a component to help us find belonging in safe spaces at home, in school and in the community. With such skills, we all learn to appreciate diversity, equity, and inclusion. This empowers each of us to weave our creativity, inspiration, and belonging into a beautiful tapestry of living.

6 Feet Apart can become a tool for you to understand more about yourself and to create 6 Feet Apart Teams of belonging with

one another. With your teacher's permission, you can create a 6 Feet Apart Team in your classroom. You can learn from each other, from your teacher and from the administrators in your school. The 6 Feet Apart Virtual Museum gives you the guidelines to begin the process. After you complete this book, go to the Virtual Museum to help you create your 6 Feet Apart Team of belonging. As the 6 Feet Apart Team explores their own emotions in this book, they weave their creativity, inspiration and belonging into a tapestry of living. You can follow this example so you can create your own tapestry. We wish you luck, love and belonging.

Dr. Sally A. Baas
School Psychologist, Professor, Author
President, Tapestry Intergenerational Education Foundation

The Historical Context of Covid 19

The 6 Feet Apart Team believes that they have a message to share with the world. During the 1918 pandemic, teenagers suffered and had challenges. Now, during the 2020 pandemic, the 6 Feet Apart Team has wanted to document their stories and yours, so history will never forget these times. I too believe they have a message. I remember well when Noah spoke the following words to me, his grandmother, one rainy, cold March day. I knew they had to be remembered...

"We are stuck at home.

Safe at home but not happy to be isolated and quarantined.

Living the same life day after day

Anxious about the future

Afraid of what is happening

Angry at what I don't have

Sad about my new lifestyle."

As Noah wrote this book, and the 6 Feet Apart Team created their stories, pictures, poems and music, there was something more to think about than loss during COVID– what we don't have, and what isn't working for us. And this too needed to be documented for historical context. The 6 Feet Apart Team was gaining from their connection and they all wanted to help other teenagers. They knew they couldn't fix the situation and make COVID go away, but they could understand more about how they could help other teenagers. This became an important component. They wanted each of you, as teenagers, to feel better about your situation if you could. This needs to be documented too. For they were not only teenagers writing a book, they were doing it to help others. For historical context, the need to help one another in challenging times, by teenagers for teenagers, is a unique concept. One that can go down in history as a model for others.

Books are now being written about COVID, and this one, by teenagers can be included among them. For as teenagers, they too have been living through history. This is a time none of us, across the world, will ever forget. It has been a time of anxiety, fear, anger, and sadness. Yes, and some happiness too. It is a time where these teenagers have explored their emotions so they understand something more about themselves and others.

Teenagers across the world have been experiencing the same things — whether they live in the United States, China, Australia, Romania, or any country in the entire world. All teenagers can be connected to one another by this virus. Noah and the 6 Feet Apart Team wrote this book during the worst of the pandemic, when thousands were dying and it became the story of their experience during this time in history.

It was particularly written for those teens who have and are experiencing the pains of this virus. Teenagers especially can share their feelings with one another. It is a documentation for others in years to come so they can understand what life was like at the height of the coronavirus.

The 6 Feet Apart Team created an unusual virtual teenage bond which has taken each of them on a journey into a new awareness. They came together with a united belief to help others through this book. They are friends who met online, through Zoom, texts, phone conversations and emails. Their bond helped them through the crisis. They will stay connected, I am sure, and continue to help other teenagers face COVID 19 and other losses. They are learning from one another and that continues to grow.

I want to thank all of the 6 Feet Apart Team. You have been my teacher and have shown me that teenagers today have the power, when united, to make incredible civic change. We need your strength, your views and your hope to lead us forward. Let's all activate our inner power of healing so we can help ourselves and others during traumatic events. Each of you can become part of the 6 Feet Apart Team. Gather together. Write your stories; share your history. Join 6 Feet Apart. We all belong.

Through the eyes of the next generation, I hope we all can gain from this 6 Feet Apart Team's optimism and laughter and love for life. To a hopeful future…

Susan Shapiro
Noah's Grandmother
Health Consultant
Author
"Kindness is my most important word!"

An Important Message For Teenagers

This is written to all teenagers who have read this book. We believe it is important for you to understand some of the mental health concerns you might hear about the pandemic. We all have dealt with a new normal. This 6 Feet Apart Team wrote this book as they experienced COVID. Several of them worked with mental health professionals, learning about mental health. Coincidentally they found there is research behind what they wrote in this book and it may interest you to understand some of it. All of the emotions they felt are normal, but because COVID went on for so long, and because no one anywhere in the world was spared, some may have experienced depression, extreme fear and feelings of hopelessness. You might also hear the word trauma. It has been used in the mental health profession. Let us explain it to you.

Trauma is a word that many have associated with COVID 19 and it is important to understand the reason this word is being used and why you don't have to fear it. Trauma is defined as an emotional response to a terrible event, so for many of us, this pandemic fits the definition. Trauma can occur during the event or after. During the event, people can feel extreme emotional reactions. In this case, anxiety was a dominating factor in the beginning of the pandemic for many adults followed by fear, anger and extreme sadness. Isolation was also a key emotion many people felt. Teenagers felt fear more than anxiety from the Survey the teens shared with you.

Some researchers have classified COVID as mass trauma because it is the same event and has traumatized large numbers of people across the globe. It doesn't have the intensity of a violent war, but it has its consequences. It has visible and invisible consequences related to it. The disease itself is visible, but the spread of it is invisible and so is the slow deterioration that has occurred for so many. For some there are massive changes – for others there aren't. We all have a lens in which we see our world, and now it has changed. Thousands, millions have been traumatized.

Now, after the event, some people may deny their feelings, wanting them to go away. They don't want to talk or think about COVID. Sometimes emotions are just too challenging. But there are those who may get depressed, have flashbacks that you are isolated once again, or get angry without cause. Some of you may get physical symptoms like headaches or stomach problems. It's hard to tell who will experience it. Many factors come into play on who will feel what. You don't have to fear that these negative feelings may happen. There are ways to deal with them. For some, COVID has challenged them but they could adapt. But if you are one of those teens who had unusual challenges - where your family was really at odds with one another, or you lost someone to COVID, or a friend got really sick, or that you were involved with political dissension, these situations can be harder to get over. This virus attacks every part of who you are as teenagers: your social life, your family life, your learning environment, and your hobbies, sports, and life outside of school. Your social, emotional, mental and spiritual lives have been touched. There are ways for you to get the help you need.

COVID 19 will end. When you read this, it may have ended. But whether or not it is over, the big questions are, "Should you think about what happened to all of us? Should we forget it and move on? We have been so immersed in it, and for some, it is the last thing we want to think about, so do we need to talk about it? Do we need to deal with it?

Forgetting the pandemic may work for some of you, but it has changed all of our lives. If we understand what occurred, if we deal with our emotions and take preventive measures, we can reduce the negative impact some of us might feel. Forgetting it may be okay to some, and a disservice to others. The 6 Feet Apart Team created the Virtual Museum for you to tell your story. Whether it was one of positive, negative, both, your story is important to hear. The more we can examine the emotions of teens during this event, the more we can help those who need the help, and understand how to better deal with such situations in the future.

Each of you can become resilient as you understand what has occurred. We hope this book gives you resources to create a new wave of energy that brings on happiness. If you are dealing with any of these challenging emotions, and you can't find happiness, ask for help. Ask your school psychologist, counselor, or teacher. This is a sign of resilience and strength when you know you need help and you ask for it. You are no different from many other teens. You are not alone in this COVID challenge.

By Simona Baciu, Dr. Sally and Susan Shapiro

The Research Behind 6 Feet Apart
Teachers and Parents: Please read!
By Edie Myhre

ACE, Adverse Childhood Experiences, is a disease caused by trauma. It affects young children. We can look at ACE research and hope that this book can help students and teachers understand more about their feelings and how to deal with them during this pandemic. Understanding our feelings, as suggested in 6 Feet Apart, is a start to prevent emotional problems that may occur because of this pandemic.

After researching trauma and adverse childhood experiences, I gained an awareness that ACE could be affecting students across the world by this pandemic and it is even right here in my school and in my neighborhood. ACE is caused by trauma. If a student is traumatized by an event, they can get emotional symptoms that can affect them in school and in their overall life. This situation is occurring during COVID. It is a traumatic event for many of us. It is not something that exists outside of my world. And I believe it needs to be more than an occasional conversation.

Based on the research I have done and continue to do, ACE affects all of us. 70% of the participants from an original ACE study were Caucasian and from college educated households. This point stuck with me, because stereotypically, I would not have taken this disease as something in my neighborhood where children from seemingly well-balanced homes on the surface are affected by Adverse Childhood Experiences. It is easy to think of them as somewhere other than where I live or as kids who had something blatantly wrong, or came from another place where students don't have the same benefits as me.

Now though many of us are in the same situation. We have experienced COVID and this has been traumatizing to us as teenagers. But we shouldn't just do nothing about it. We can explore our emotions and understand more about how we are feeling. We can help combat this pandemic experience through education and information given directly to teachers and community organizations about Adverse Childhood Experiences and its wide range of people it affects.

When working with students, it is important to know that ACE cannot be overlooked because a student's life goes beyond the basic facts a teacher might know about them. Understanding this disease, and its complexity could be an effective means for teachers to think about the challenging behaviors that students may face. The importance of researching and developing concepts to help students, teachers and the community is needed so the help, care, and treatment is not delayed. I suspect there are great numbers of improper diagnosis' such as ADHD or Asthma labeled to students who might have ACE. We cannot compartmentalize or label students who may be susceptible to Adverse Childhood Experiences.

We need to make sure the information we give is age appropriate. This book was written by teenagers for teenagers. As teenagers we do not know how this pandemic will affect us. We cannot grasp the possible concept of trauma or the damaging effects it could have on our body for the rest of our life.

ACE research is for young children so we are saying that even though we are teenagers, we can be affected by this pandemic. We may not consider ourselves children, but I believe ACE can apply to us as well. Even the research that has been done, for children, cannot hurt us. For us to deal with the pandemic can only help us feel better about ourselves. No young child can have control of a situation which would ultimately give them an unhealthy amount of stress hormones that are then released into their bodies, changing the anatomy of their amygdala, and ultimately changing the way that their DNA is read and transcribed.

The ACE research lends itself to teachers and parents. Parents should let their physicians know that this pandemic may have affected their children. It is impossible for children to understand so it must be the parents, medical field, psychologists and others who support children to become aware of ACE and find ways to deal with it. I do believe that older students can learn about this disease when taught through researched and highly developed curricula.

A wide variety of health problems from the trauma can occur but teachers need to consider options if they see their students with the symptoms. Students might feel comfortable seeking support or help, if they know that this could improve their positive well-being. There are a wide range of behaviors that make up adverse childhood experiences such as divorce, abuse, or parent incarceration. Therefore, even something as common as a divorce, should not be looked over, because it could cause trauma if not handled appropriately. We are hoping to make teachers and parents aware that educating students at the appropriate age on adverse childhood experiences, and teaching them how to be emotionally and situationally aware can aid in earlier diagnosis and hopefully reduce the long-term effects of the traumatic experience.

Last but not least, I have learned about the importance of using a multistep process as the means to truly diagnose, help and heal children who have experienced or are experiencing trauma. ACE must be developed for all levels of educational awareness. For example, this education would ideally start at home, with parents who take their children to get regular pediatric checkups, knowing that their pediatricians will have their children screened. But I personally take proactive support to create community organizations. Community programs can build awareness and make information available to children and families who have experienced trauma.

Proactive steps are beginning to emerge as the reality of this disease escalates, especially now during COVID times. Research is suggesting preschool enrichment programs that support children at a young age, and also parent training and accessible mental illness treatment that can help break the trauma to trauma cycle. It is important to have programs within a community for every "stage of life". This will help identify children who have endured trauma and prevent situations "spiraling" out of control at earlier stages. During this COVID crisis, it certainly is time to address these concerns. This book can hopefully help teenagers. It can also address the needs for parents to be aware of the trauma we all are facing. And if anyone has younger brothers or sisters, ACE is the awareness to help all of us recognize how trauma affects us.

The Five Emotions Survey

The format uses a Google questionnaire format.

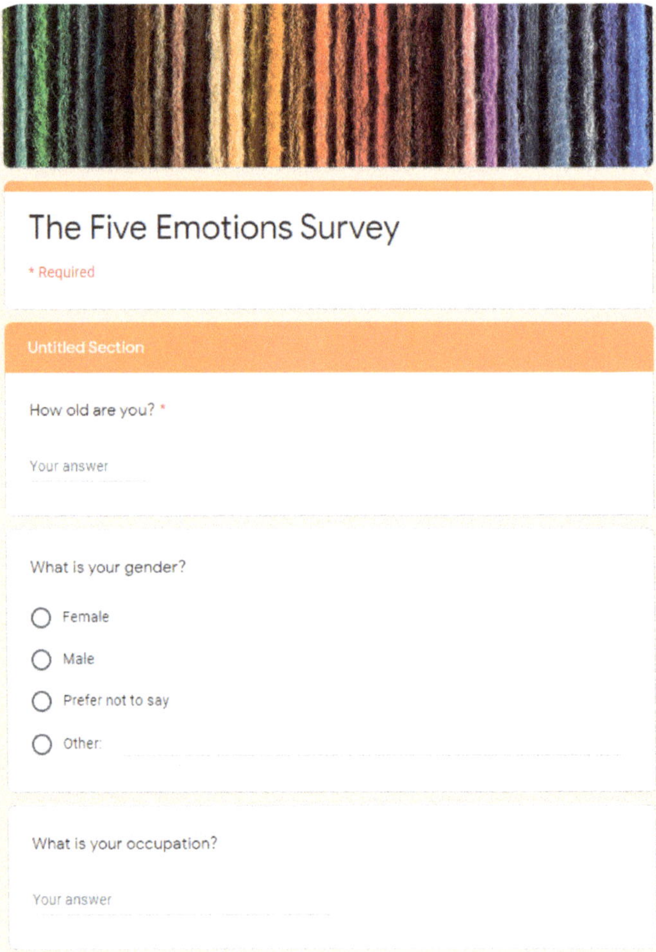

The Five Emotions Survey

* Required

Untitled Section

How old are you? *

Your answer

What is your gender?

○ Female

○ Male

○ Prefer not to say

○ Other:

What is your occupation?

Your answer

What country do you live in? *

Your answer

To what extent do you feel FEAR due to the coronavirus? *

	1	2	3	4	5	
Not at all	○	○	○	○	○	A lot

To what extent do you feel ANXIOUS due to the coronavirus? *

	1	2	3	4	5	
Not at all	○	○	○	○	○	A lot

To what extent do you feel ANGRY due to the coronavirus? *

	1	2	3	4	5	
Not at all	○	○	○	○	○	A lot

To what extent do you feel HAPPY due to the coronavirus? *

	1	2	3	4	5	
Not at all	○	○	○	○	○	A lot

To what extent do you feel SAD due to the coronavirus? *

	1	2	3	4	5	
Not at all	○	○	○	○	○	A lot

Which emotion is having the biggest impact on you? *

○ Anxiety

○ Fear

○ Happiness

○ Anger

○ Sadness

○ Other:

What makes you feel that way? *

Your answer

What brings you the most meaning during the coronavirus outbreak? *

○ Family

○ Friends

○ Surfing the web

○ Being alone

○ Reading

○ Exercising

○ Other:

Thanks for your help! If you'd like to learn about my book when it is published, please provide your email here:

Your answer

Back   Submit

Participating Countries and Occupations

The countries participating in the Survey included: United States of America, Romania, Portugal, Rwanda, Germany, Canada, Switzerland, Ireland, United Kingdom, Cyprus, Australia, China, Colombia, Czech Republic, Israel, Spain, Palestine, New Zealand, France.

The range of occupations was incredible. We received responses from: Mental Health Worker, Janitor, Community Residence Counselor, Clinical Psychology Research Assistant, Engineer, Global Public Servant (WEF), Teacher, Retired Teacher, Project Manager, Antreprenor, Project Manager, Vocational Rehabilitation Counselor, Translator, Reporter, Nurse, Civil Engineer, Theatre Creator/Community Artist, Sales Professional, Data Scientist, Account manager, World Economic Forum Employee, Artist, Musician, Community Lead, Asia Pacific (WEF), Psychologist, Policy Advisor in Government, Economist, Environment Project Manager, World Economic Forum, Driver, Homemaker, Security Analyst, University Writing Instructor, Catholic Priest , Researcher, PhD researcher, Certified Vocational Evaluator, Scientist, Relationship Manager, Lawyer, Facilitator, Chef, Speech therapist, Yoga teacher, Journalist, Banker, School Counselor, Doctor, Secretary , Inclusion Consultant for young children in need of Special Education, Railroad track inspector, Maze Designer, and last, but not least a Grumpy old man.

Countries Participating

Here's a map that shows where those who took the Survey came from...

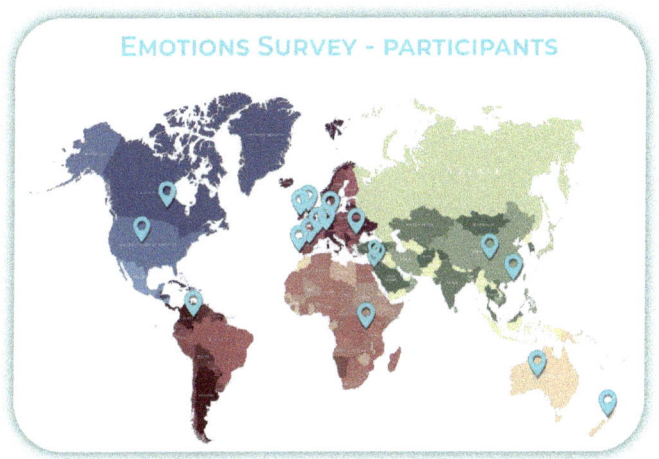

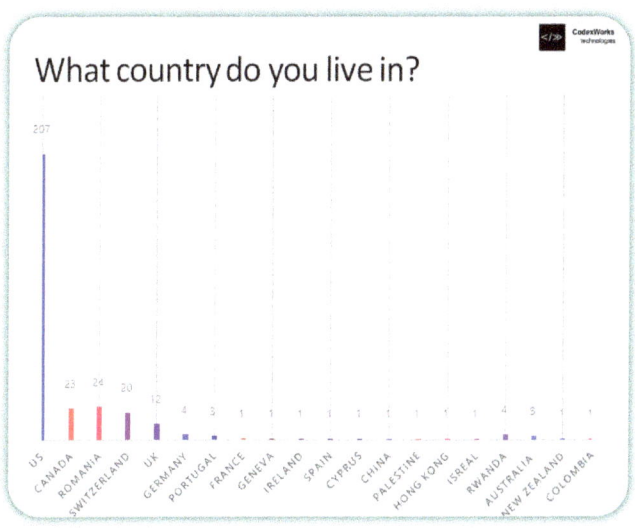

Gender

Gender distribution of the participants

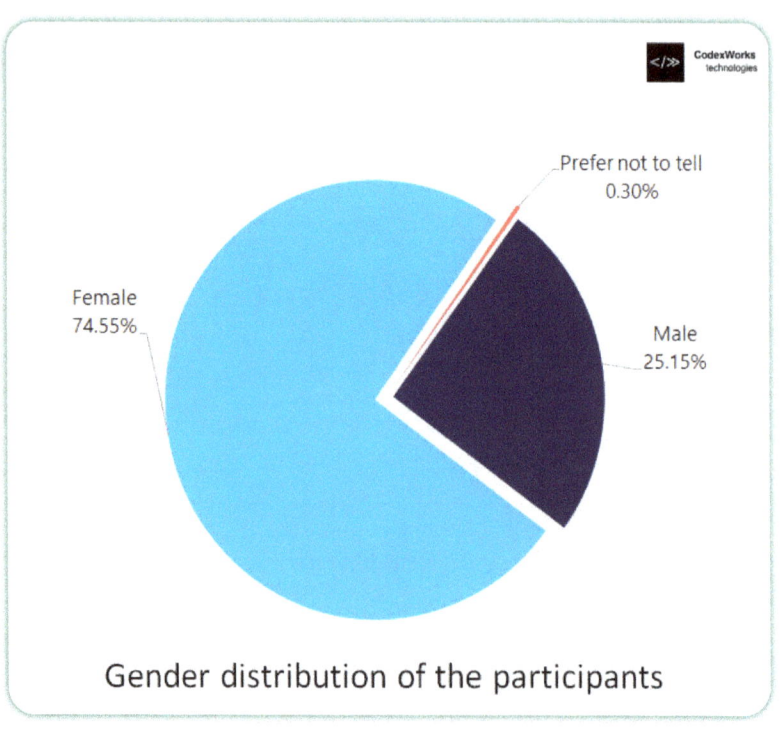

Gender distribution of the participants

Data Results

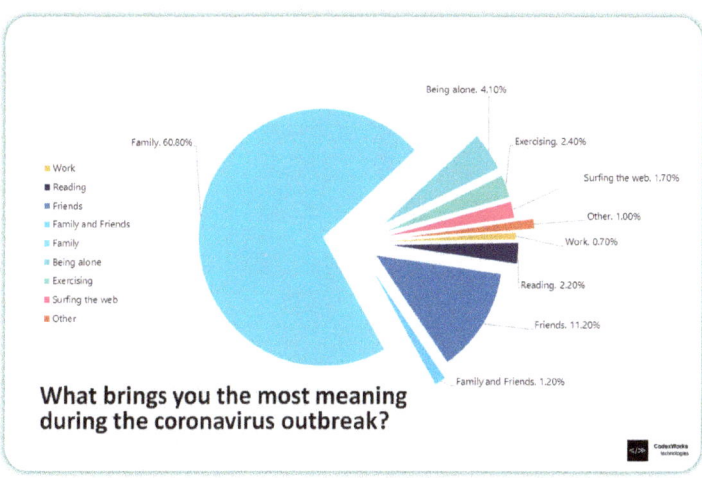

What brings you the most meaning during the coronavirus outbreak?

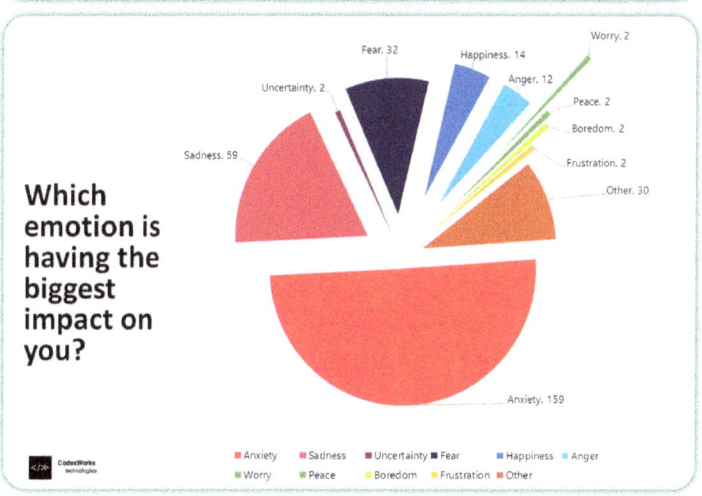

Which emotion is having the biggest impact on you?

Anxiety

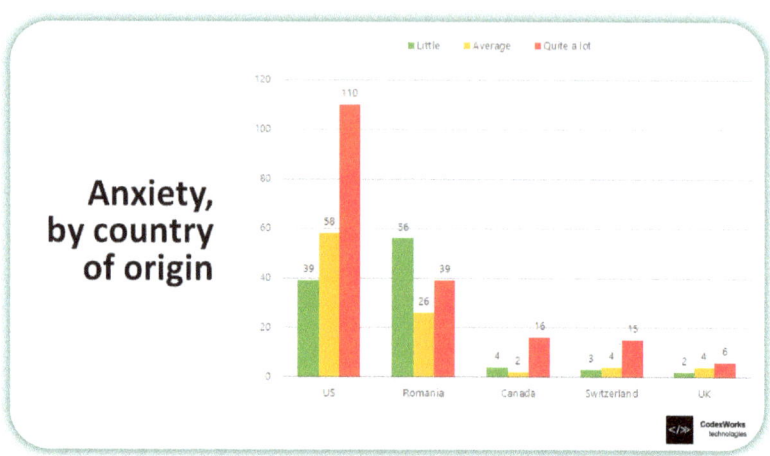

The chart shows that people in the USA, Canada, Switzerland and the UK felt quite a lot of anxiety. In Romania the anxiety level was lower.

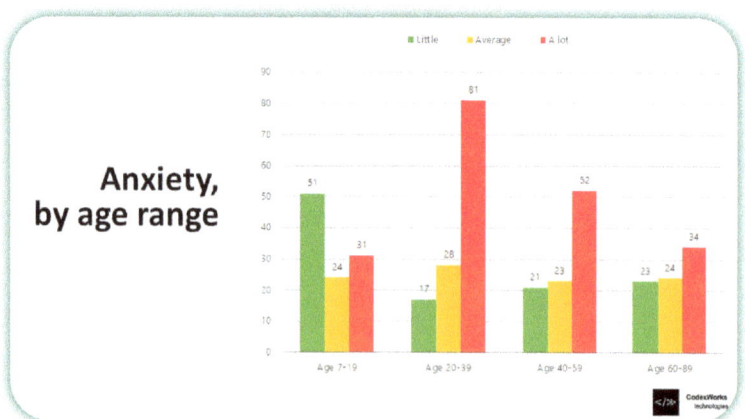

According to these charts, the anxiety level of teenagers was a lot lower than those in their 20s and above.

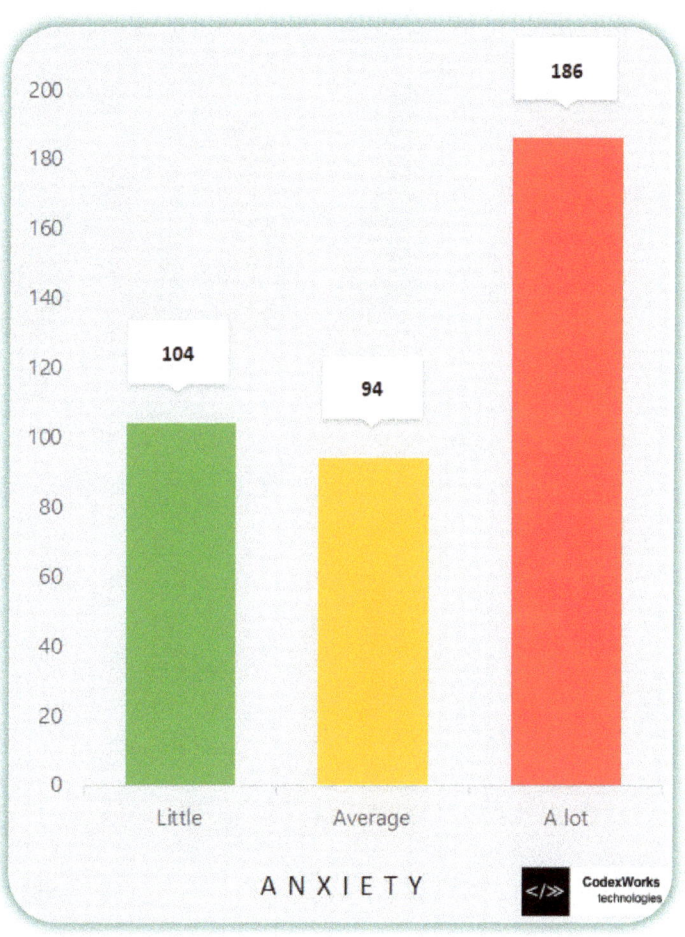

Fear

Fear, by age range

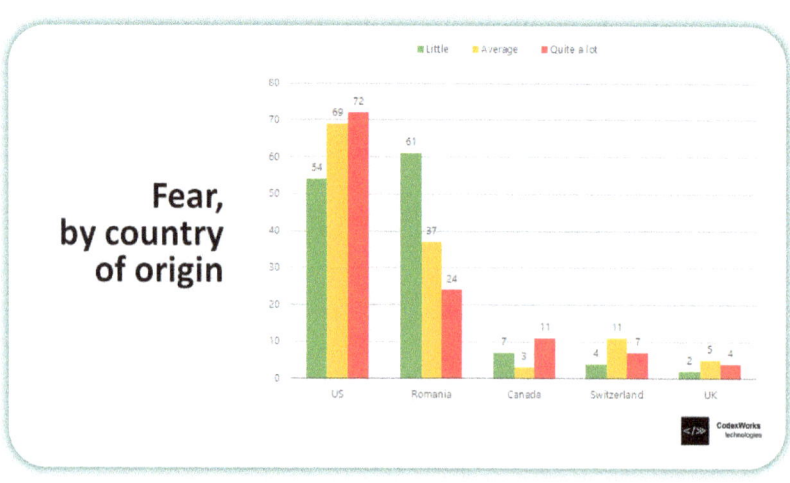

Fear, by country of origin

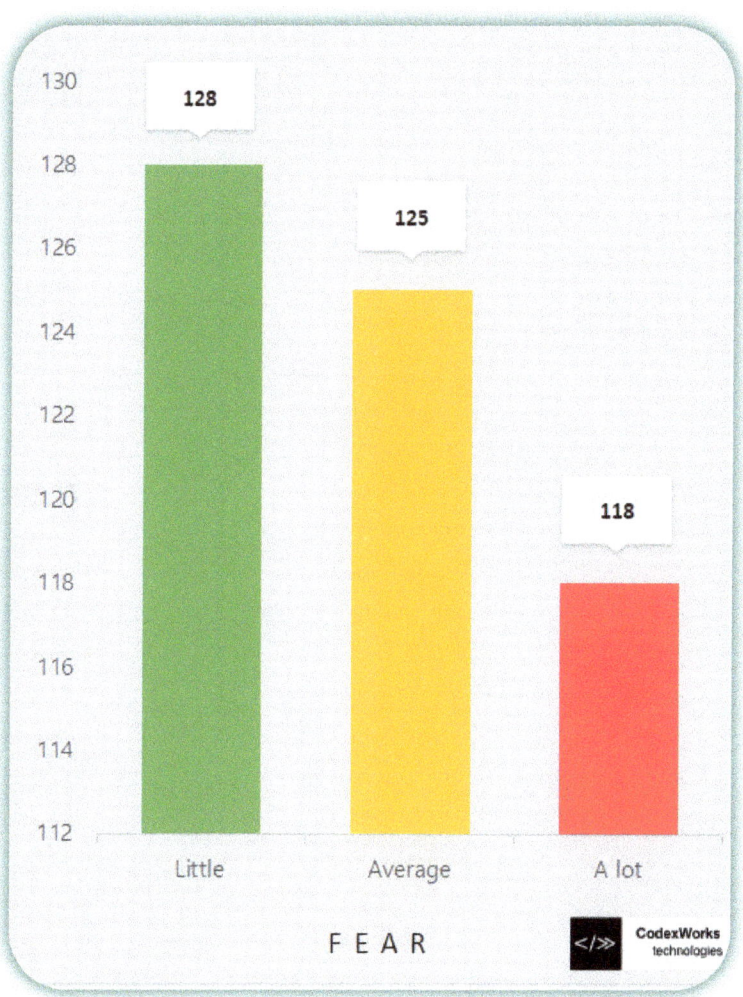

Anger

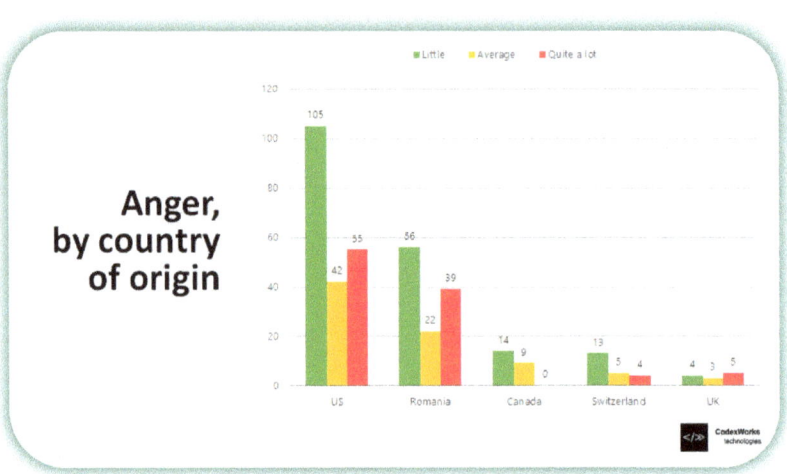

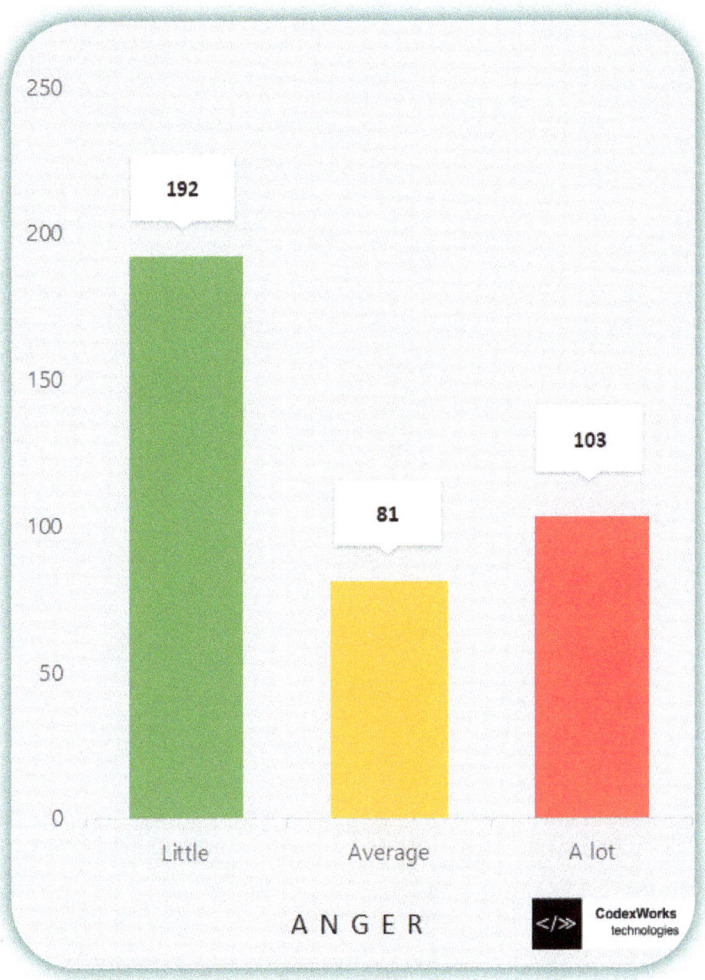

Sadness

Sadness, by age range

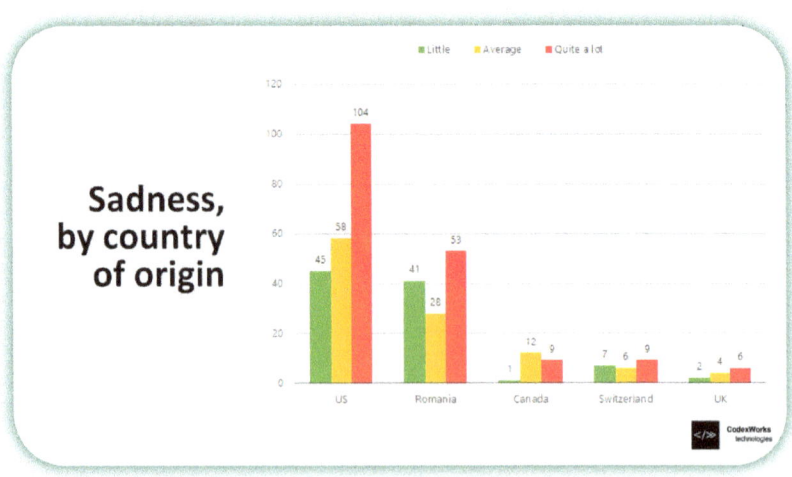

Sadness, by country of origin

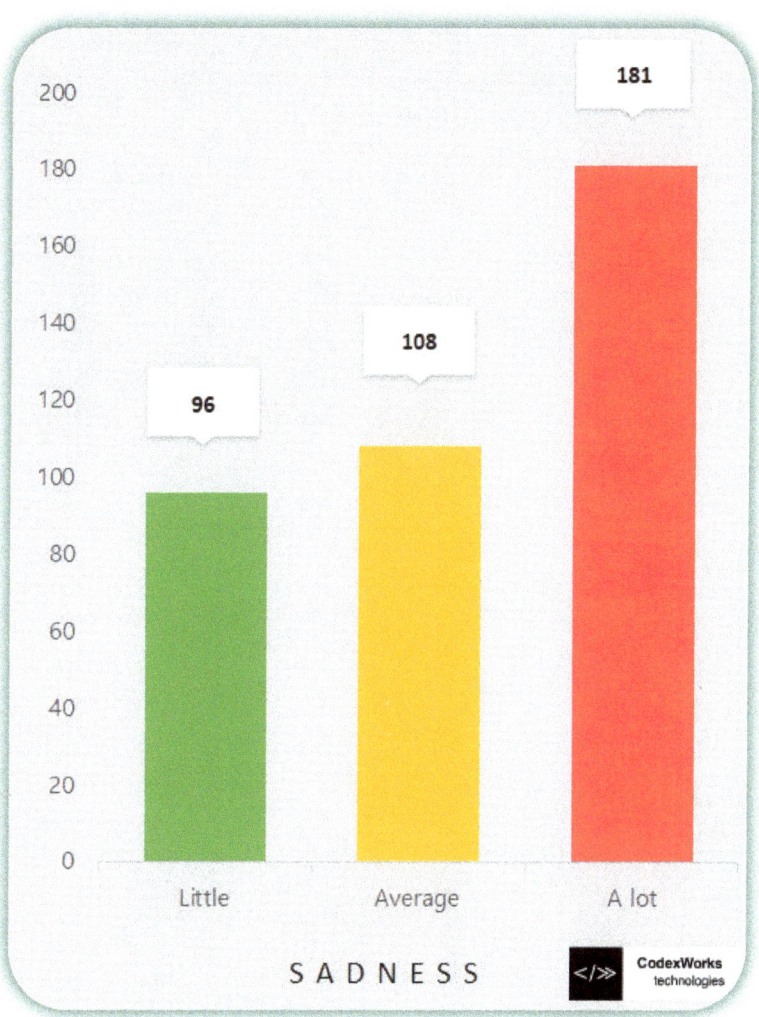

Happiness

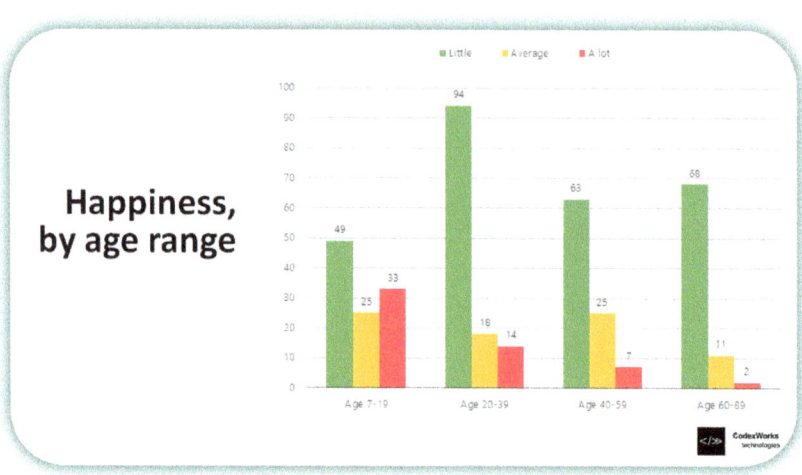

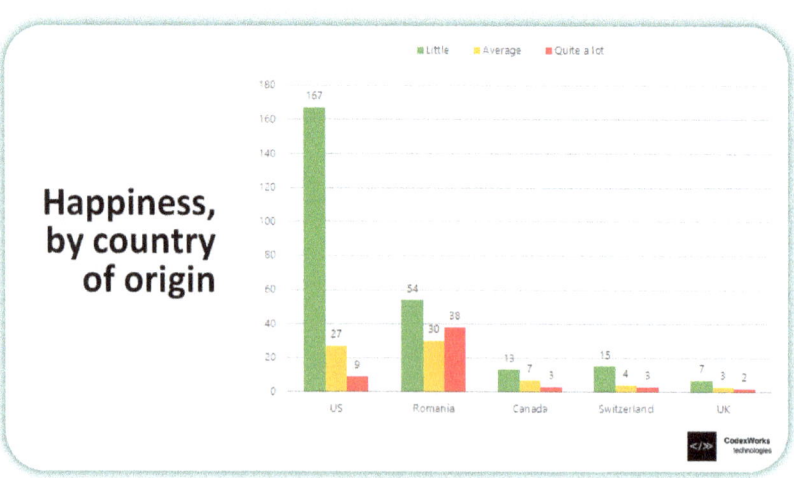

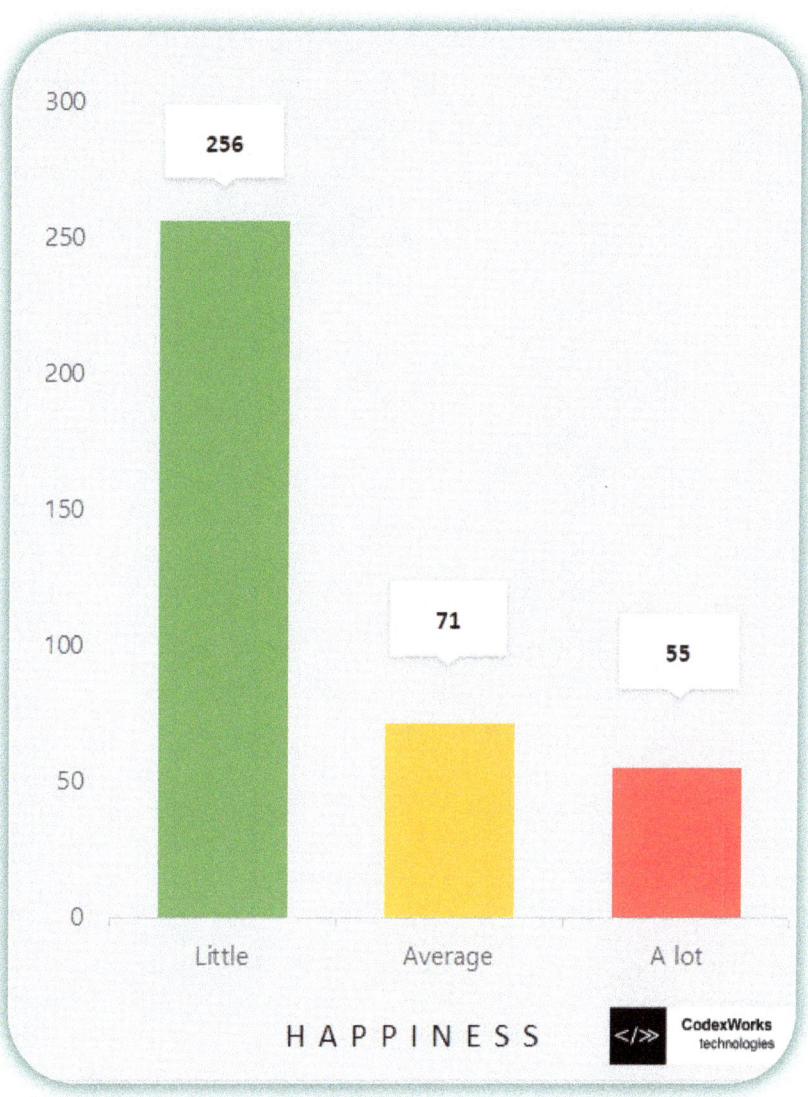

Contributing Coaches/Authors/Editors

Susan Shapiro

Ms. Susan Shapiro is an author, motivational speaker, education and training specialist with comprehensive experience in teaching, teacher training, curriculum development and programming. She has designed, developed and implemented life skills training programs for students and adults that have impacted the teaching and training of educators in thousands of schools across the globe. She has co-authored three books with Dr. Peter Killeen, Law Enforcement Professional on mindfulness, resilience and well-being, called **Operation Longevity: A Mindful Approach to Wellness and Resilience for Law Enforcement in the 21st Century** and a follow-up for **First Responders** specifically dealing with Mental and Spiritual Self-Care. Susan Shapiro has published a book with McFarland Publishers, **The Curtain Rises: Oral Histories of the Fall of Communism in Eastern Europe**. She has also written her memoir, **The Perseverance of Hope**, her personal story comparing cultures in different countries. Her training materials, books, curricula, and student planners are used world-wide in schools, libraries, and universities.

Dr. Sally A. Baas directs the Southeast Asian Teacher Program and Hmong Culture and Language Program, at Concordia University, in St. Paul, MN. She is a Past President of the National Association of School Psychologists. Professionally, she is a school psychologist, professor, author, and international education consultant, with a focus on wellbeing, diversity, equity, and advocacy. She facilitates national and international work to build student's inner wealth and education. She is President of Tapestry Intergenerational Education Foundation.

Simona Baciu

Simona Baciu is an innovative and visionary leader in education. She is a recipient of the British International School Lifetime Award and holder of the Custodian of the Romanian Crown Medal, awarded for her outstanding contribution to education.

At the beginning of the 1990's, as a teacher in a state school in Romania, Simona decided to start a school that would introduce change in the prevailing system and make a difference in the lives of students.

Happy Kids Kindergarten was opened in 1993 in one of the rooms of her family's small apartment. This is how Transylvania College, today a well-known and prestigious institution with over 700 students, was born.

Simona is an educator, speaker, author, trainer, and consultant for the improvement of education in Romania and abroad. As a Board Member of Round Square, Global Connections, Princess Margareta of Romania Foundation, and TedX Eroilor, Simona acts as a global agent of change for education. She has authored numerous articles and spoken at both national and international events and conferences promoting education for the 21st century, incorporating social-emotional learning, mindfulness, and well-being. Simona believes that education should cultivate and nurture a love for life-long learning in everyone, while keeping a curious mind, an open heart and a caring soul for the world in which we live.

To The Best Technology Company in The World!!! The 6 Feet Apart Team Is So Grateful to You and Your Hard Work. You Are Fabulous and You Will Forever Be Our Colleagues and Friends. Thank You from The 6 Feet Apart Team and The Coaches!!!!!

CodexWorks Technologies is a team of young, ambitious, driven people, specialized in business process automation and web applications development. We are currently located in Cluj-Napoca, Romania and offer custom software development services. We also work on Artificial Intelligence projects and healthcare software. Our team is the main factor of success, and we are deeply passionate about our work. And so is our involvement with The 6 Feet Apart **Project.**

The current global situation is testing our social solidarity above all else. The self-isolation and quarantines we experienced in 2020, along with all the rules and regulations about wearing masks and social distancing, were pattern-breaking for most of us, and we all felt like it is easier to let go of our usual routines of self-care and let our energy and motivational levels dwindle. Each of us needs emotional support. We all need to be heard.

Our Contribution to **6 Feet Apart**: Given the circumstances, we are extremely excited about The 6 Feet Apart project initiative, and we have felt honored to take part in its implementation. Our contribution was the development of the three modules that facilitate the interaction with the project:

- the Website,

- the Platform,

- the 3D Virtual Museum

Our goal is to help students benefit from a genuine interaction with everything **6 Feet Apart** has to offer. It really is something that we wholeheartedly believe in and could not be more eager to see it to fruition.

Special thanks to **Babeş-Bolyai University** of Cluj-Napoca for the support offered in this project!

Our collaboration resulted in an incredible team of student developers, who played a huge role in the creation of the modules:

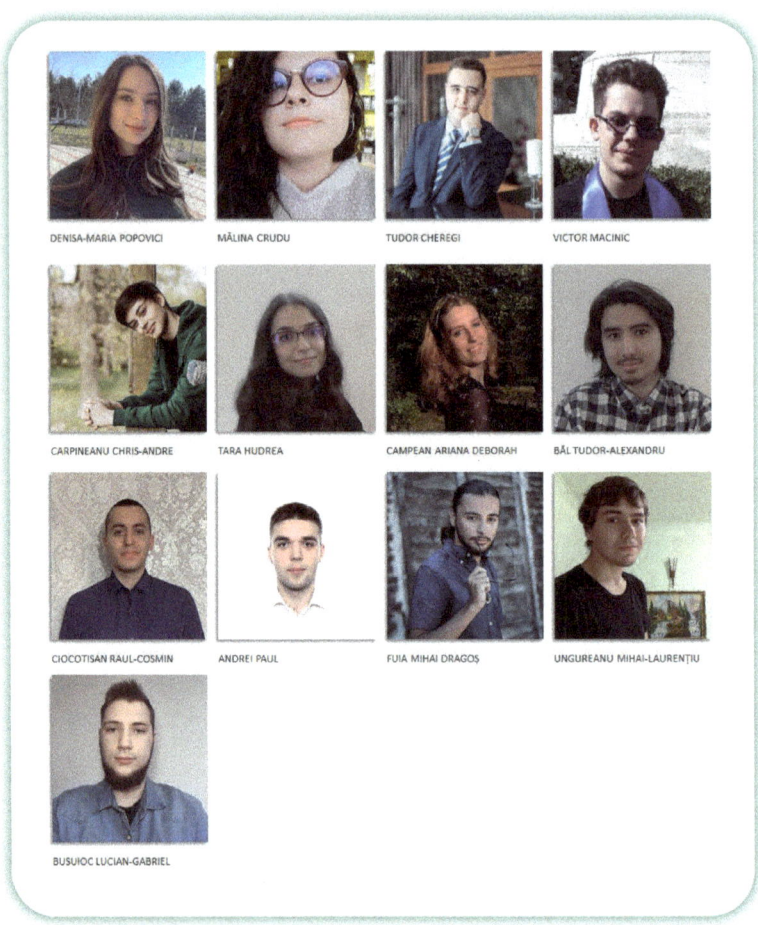

Get in touch with us: codexworks.com

Stay Safe. Stay healthy. Stay happy.

CodexWorks Team

Global Passport

In Gratitude

To The Many Incredible People Who
Have Participated In This Book

From The 6 Feet Apart Team:

Dear Susan,

The 6 ft apart team wants to thank you from the bottom of our hearts, for your kindness, understanding and support. It was so nourishing to be lifted up by you throughout this whole project. Thank you for the safe space you created. You truly made the team an environment for all of us to genuinely talk about our emotions and that was such an important addition to our creativity, our honest thoughts. Thank her for being the mind and spirit behind this project, and spearheading ideas and helping to get the ball rolling while also being in a facilitator position and motivating and supporting all of us. We loved how you cared so much for each one of us teens. Susan, we thank you and are so appreciative of all you do.

Love,
The teens

To CODEX, our new Romanian colleagues, who donated their time and energy to make this work. Florentin and George, you have been patient and thoughtful, ultimately making the 6 Feet Apart Virtual Museum see the light of day. You Are Amazing and We Want to Come Meet You in Cluj. You Are Welcome to The United States. Come and Meet Us Here Too. Your skills, your kindness, your organization, your everything has made our Virtual Museum a reality. We hope it serves teenagers, parents and educators around the world. We hope they all get to experience a "touch of Romanian" kindness, intellect, skills, and abilities. We want to also extend our sincerest gratitude to the computer science interns in Romania. You have been so accommodating, understanding and have continued to amaze us with your creativity and ideas. It has been magical to witness all of you bring us teens' visions to life. An infinite amount of gratitude to the entire CODEX team

Thank You to Dr. Sally: It was a miracle that you showed up in our lives. You are brilliant with a huge heart and each of us has felt special. You are our role model and we thank you for your time, effort and belief in us.

Thank You to Simona Baciu and her incredible energy to make this project come alive in Romania. She has contributed to this book in so many ways. As a coach, as a reader, organizing us so the book flows, as a dear friend to all of us, as a colleague to Susan and Sally and thank you for believing in us.

Thank you to the Think Up Team in Romania. Without all of you, we would not have been able to expand our project and make 6 Ft Apart an international initiative. Thank you so much for believing in us, supporting, and challenging us by bringing each of your brilliant minds to the table to make our project better.

Thank You So Much to Dr. Joanne Cashman for your investment into each and everyone of our 6 Feet Apart Team members. Getting to study under you and work with you has been a privilege. Your support of this project has been insurmountable, and your network and mental health knowledge have been an intrical part to developing 6 Feet Apart.

We extend a huge thank you to Gabriela Secosan. We are so grateful for the time you have spent with our 6 Feet Apart Team and dedication you have shown to helping our project succeed. Without you, we would not have been able to create and roll out our webinar successfully. Your caring personality and positive energy helped take our project to the next level!

Thank you to Edie Myhre who took the role of leadership for

the 6 Feet Apart Team. Edie spent hours organizing the team, helping everyone get the material in on time, worrying about the concerns of each member, and so much more. Edie's diligence and commitment helped to make this book all that it has become. The Team is grateful to you Edie!!!

Thank you to Professor Rui Wu and Professor Stephen Moysey for your help with the Survey and for allowing your computer science students to take this project on as a classroom assignment at Eastern Carolina University.

Thank you so much to all of our Board Members who have donated their resources and time, and dedicated themselves to making sure all of our dreams come true. All of you motivate us to continue our work on this project everyday! The Board is made up of 11 individuals who have a variety of backgrounds, Special Education, School Psychology, University professors from several countries and US states, and those representing their own foundations.

From Noah:

To My Parents...Thank you to my parents! Whether you asked me how it was going or what we're doing with the book, you cared about what was happening. I am grateful. And I love you both.

To Dr. Sally:

You have made this possible through your positive energy and your knowledge and your kindness. You have been my mentor and I am so grateful for what you have given to all of us.

To The 6 Feet Apart Team - You are extraordinary. We come from different backgrounds, different ages, different life experiences, yet we united into a team where judgement was not a label - negativity didn't exist and positivism, belief in one another, and joy dominated. We laughed on Zoom together. We shared our best efforts. This is a framework that can be duplicated because together we accomplished so much, and we tried to live the principles within the book. Finding the positive in one another, giving to a project to help others, and serving something bigger than ourselves is the message most obvious to me. Our 6 Feet Apart Team is proof that a positive team can work together. I wish each of you the best and hope we stay in touch.

To My Brothers... Zach and Liam, even though you can be very annoying at times, I am super glad to have you as my brothers. Liam, It's very cool to see the creations you construct. Zach, playing basketball or talking about anything with you, is great. I love you

To My Cousins:

Jake and Annie... Being cousins with you guys is the best. Even though we don't live very close to each other, the times that we either came to your house or you came to ours have been so fun. I can't wait to see you soon. You're the best.

To Joan Myhre...You're amazing to talk to and very relatable. I'm so thankful that I got to know you through this book. Like my Nana said, you have a gift for visualizing and brainstorming. I learned a lot from you. From Susan...you are amazing to me and Noah. Your ability to brainstorm, visualize what needs to get done, and be part of our 6 Feet Apart Team is a highlight for me. You have been my friend for close to 50 years and I feel blessed to have you in my life. Thank you for being part of this book. For us to work together, each having a grandchild involved (Edie's grandmother) has been special.

To Dr. Peter Killeen...You're so kind, compassionate, and loving to all. Hearing your stories about 9/11 were eye opening. I will never forget them. From Susan...It has been my pleasure working with you and learning from your belief in finding one's higher purpose. As a friend and colleague, you have changed my life, adding much understanding and deeper meaning. Thank you, Peter.

From The 6 Feet Apart Team:

Simona Baciu - Thank you for brainstorming and spending time helping us to create this book. And thank you for your kind words in the Foreword. What an incredible opportunity for The 6 Feet Apart team to get to know you. WE WILL ALL COME TO CLUJ!!!

Gabriela Secosan...This book has a completely new life because of the work you have done with the 6 Feet Apart Team. The webinars add tremendous opportunities and your skill in teaching all of us how to work together online is amazing. Noah, Edie and Samantha talk about you as though you have been their friend forever. Thank you and we hope your energy, so positive and uplifting, travels across the globe.

Zsuzsa Magyary - Your ability to help all of us understand the data of the Survey is such a great addition to this book. We all thank you - the entire 6 Feet Apart Team for helping us simplify the Survey so we all can understand it. We all would love to meet you someday. We know you live in Cluj - Napoca, Romania, but that's just an ocean away! Thank you Zsuzsa!

Corina Chiorean - has been a terrific help in all aspects of 6 Feet Apart, but the most help has been learning how she chooses a positive attitude, no matter the circumstance. She never said anything was too much for her to do and we have recognized by her attitude, that we all have a model, right in the Romanian office. Just an email away – a What's App away!!! Thank you, Corina!

Randi Goldstein - Thank you Randi for giving us Julia! Her work is phenomenal as everyone can see it within this book. But you also introduced us to other exceptional artists - Amani and Nathan. We are all grateful for your belief in this book and your help to make it come to reality.

Elyse Conner - A warm thank you to Elyse Conner, Adjunct Professor of Mindfulness at the University of Virginia in Charlottesville, Virginia. She offered techniques to me on mindfulness and meditation.

She is the founder of the Open Door Wellness consultancy, which creates individualized programming for clients to optimize their well-being. She teaches mindfulness and yoga with the Contemplative Sciences Center and Curry School of Education at the University of Virginia. T

To Carol Barash who helped the team understand the importance of good storytelling. She started Story2 where she has taught thousands of people how to tell their stories. We are so grateful for the time you spent with us. If any of you want to master storytelling you can email Carol at: getstarted@story2.com. Thank you for your friendship and your skills.

Cheers to the best Team Leader: Edie Myhre

We as a team would like to acknowledge our team Leader, Miss Edie Myhre. Writing this is her best friend Cassandra on behalf of the team. I have been friends with Edie for about 7 years now and I have gotten to know her quite well. This project only made me learn more amazing traits about her. To narrow down the list of positive adjectives that describe Edie, I chose three that she feels best represent herself. She described herself in her Key Club Lieutenant Governor bio with these three words: inquisitive, outgoing, and bubbly. Edie wasn't overshooting it because if anyone meets Edie, they will see how these words describe her. She is never afraid to ask questions and dive deeper into a study or getting to know someone. Her inquisitiveness helps enhance her intelligence. Moving on to outgoing, this girl will bite the bullet and just do it. She has great judgement on what is best so if she feels good about it there is no stopping her. Finally, to bubbly which is a great way to end. You can never tell when Edie is tired because she is always fired up, ready to go. This is great energy to have on the team because she keeps everyone going with a bright attitude. To sum up, Edie is a full package and we are beyond thankful to have her as our team leader.

Now to the list of thanks ....

Thank you, Edie, for planning all the meetings and making sure things got done. This task was not easy. Getting seven teenagers' schedules to all link up was very challenging but Edie found a way to get most of us on the call. For the ones who were unable to attend she made sure to fill them in later. We would never get bored seeing a text from Edie with good intentions and never a negative message. Furthermore, we thank you for leading these meetings with clear points and a positive attitude.

Thank you for working hard with Joanne Cashman; worker for the National Association of Directors of Special Ed, organizing and interpreting the research from the Survey. Edie was thrilled to take on this task as she is interested in pursuing a career in psychology.

Thank you for making illustrations and taking photos for this book. Edie took on this duty over the summer while she was even balancing preparing for applying to colleges. Thank you for staying persistent and giving us full effort even with dealing with your personal life. Edie has so much to juggle yet she never missed a beat for this project. She is always professional. She carries on the role of being a big sister too and watches her brother while her parents are away or helps them run him around to his events.

Personally, I would like to thank Edie for getting me involved in this project. Edie called me one day and asked if I would like to draw a couple of pictures for a book and now look at all she helped me to experience. This is a one in a lifetime opportunity that I would have NEVER been able to do without her. From my heart, Edie, I thank you so much for thinking of me and setting me up for success. I can always trust you steering me in the right direction. Love You!

Lastly, thank you for being you! This book is about all of us, and if you weren't a part of it, it would never be what it is now.

With extreme love and thanks,

Noah, Asia Rae, Amani, Elif, Julia, Sam, and me Cassandra!!!

To Those Who Have Stayed Six Feet Apart

Living In A Pandemic Is Hard! For Those Who Wear

Masks And Wash Your Hands Often,

You Are Saving Others.

Thank You!

The Artwork on The Cover

By Samantha Rosser

The painting on the cover is my visual response to how COVID-19 has affected me. It displays the stress, the heartache, the despair, and the loneliness I felt during this time. I felt isolated due to the lack of social connection and emotional support.

There was a craving for social contact that I was unable to get and that made me feel like I was being put in a bubble, my own little bubble that was distanced from everyone else. Inside the bubble, you can see a figure in a crouched position. I wanted to symbolize the posture of sadness and emptiness because those feelings were very real and very present. It's like when we are sad, we want to curl up in a little ball and cry, holding our heads and waiting for the pain to be over.

The other bubble reflects a similar yet different feeling and that is lethargy. During quarantine, we had to entertain ourselves to pass time but as time went on, sleep became the default option. The position of the figure, where they are lying on their side and crouched in a sleeping position, is supposed to represent the fatigue we all felt during COVID. It's a little hard to see but there is a 3rd figure in the bottom left. I didn't color this one in like I did the others because I kind of liked the way it faded into the background. In this position, the arms are wrapped around the legs to show anxiety and fear.

To create this piece, I used ink and water for the background. Then I drew bubbles and used a coating to put around the bubble so the paint would stay inside the bubble. I used a mix of ink and water colors to paint the bubbles using the colors blue, green, and purple. I kept adding bubbles and layers of ink and water colors until I liked the composition I had made. Occasionally, I would go in with white paint to put back into the bubbles because the ink would make them too dark. The figures took a lot more time to create. I had to trace the shape of them and then go in with multiple sharpies to draw individual lines to cover the whole body shape. I actually painted this towards the end of last year (2020) for an art project about water when COVID first began, so you could say I predicted it. But seriously, these emotions: sadness, fear, anger, anxiety, and happiness are always present in our everyday life, it was just COVID that amplified it. I hope you enjoy my art and interpretation!

What's coming next....

MyndeLab

An experience for all teens...

Come and join in! This is an experience
you might only imagine in your
dreams! It's about to come true!

Enter another world. A world where you are in control. A world where you can meet other teens your age and hear their stories as you tell yours. A world where you can learn more about yourself. It's called MYNDELAB – and it's all about YOU!

MYNDELAB is a website and platform turned into a laboratory for you as teens around the world to share your stories and experiences with one another, as you explore its unusual mazelike pathways.

You will explore your surroundings and at the same time focus on your emotions. You will be able to collaborate with other teens. All of this is supported by mental health professionals and our very own maze designer, so you can acquire knowledge and skills to make effective decisions for yourself. You will have the chance to explore your feelings and at the same time, relate to other teens about your feelings.

You will be able to develop youth teams and play games, as you find your way through many different types of mazes. You will explore your way through a maze, similar to the way we all go through life, by recognizing your twisting paths and sometimes unknown outcomes. But as you go through the maze, you can change your goals and find those surprising obstacles that lead you to understand more about who you are.

Adrian Fisher is the world's leading maze designer. He is immensely imaginative and creative, and conceived the way MyndeLab works. "Young people are so important to the future of the world," he says. "When you are happy, you are open to new ideas, and enjoy discovering them. They become part of you, who you are, and how you think."

Here's some of what you may experience while you roam through MyndeLab.

Discover your wisdom and your inspiration.

You will have the chance to build your personal collection of favorite quotes. As your life unfolds from one event to the next, these quotes will ring in your ears, mold you and your life story, and shape who you become. Here are some famous ones, but you too can be famous and share yours!

"Freedom is not worth having if it does not include the freedom to make mistakes." - Mahatma Gandhi.

"Be kind whenever possible. It is always possible." - Dalai Lama.

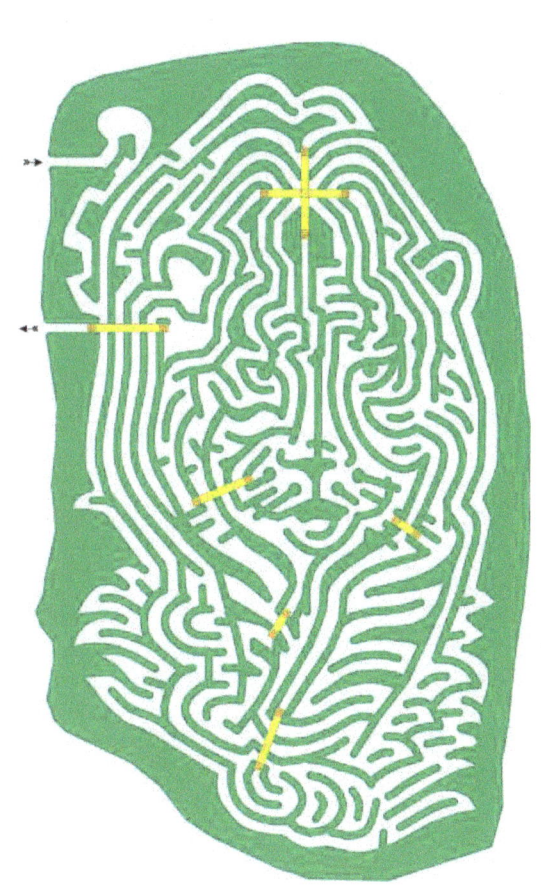

Create winning strategies for your value and livelihood.

You will understand and master your creativity skills. They are crucial for developing your mind and for you to achieve genuine added value to what you want to do in life. Let Artificial Intelligence, robots and automation take care of repetitive tasks. Make your own unique character and humanity "futureproof"!

You will be able to build your imagination. Imagination is the source of every form of human achievement. Creativity is as important now in education as literacy and we should treat it with the same status.

Discover enduring principles that will help you throughout your life.

Visit MyndeLab. ADD YOUR INSIGHT! As a teenager, it's your MyndeLab. Share your insights with the world, and benefit from the insights of other teenagers all over the world. Insights you may have thought, or insights you have come across and wish to share.

Discover TED talks - "ideas worth sharing". Incredible free online videos of tens of thousands of 18- minute talks, given by many of the finest minds on the planet.

Let art, music, beauty, nature, friendships and wonder fill your hearts and your spirits.

You as teens can fill your lives with abundance and achieve vibrant minds. The world can learn from you! You are our future.

Welcome to MYNDELAB, soon to be launched as a website platform. It's all about you and for you as TEENS!

Adrian Fisher devised the way that MyndeLab works.

He is internationally acknowledged as the world's leading maze designer. He has created over seven hundred hedge mazes, mirror mazes and labyrinths across forty two countries, winning two gold medals and setting eight Guinness World Records. He received the honour of Member of the Order of the British Empire (MBE) in the Queen's 2020 Birthday Honours, for services to International Trade and the Creative Industries.

His distinctive GEOMITICA art literally means "the Mythology of Shape" with the word Mythology referring to the stories, truths, parables and values of our societies and culture. Using exacting choices of colour, texture and pattern, each piece of art he creates is unique and yet immediately recognizable.

His landscape garden in southern England contains a hedge maze, and a folly tower with mirrored chamber and a spiral staircase leading to the battlements above.

adrian@adrianfisherdesign.com